All Wrong Turns

True (And Sometimes Twisted) Tales of
Coastal Delaware
From the Backroads to the Beaches

Bill Newcott

They're not llamas!

ISBN: 9798733619286

For Carolyn, who said, "Let's move to the beach."

CONTENTS

FOREWORD

Welcome to my book! I suppose my first order of business should be to offer a word of explanation (and, perhaps, apology) to longtime readers of *Delaware Beach Life* magazine. That's because much of what you will read between these covers draws heavily from articles first published in that fine publication.

You may as well learn how the sausage is made: The magazine's publisher, Terry Plowman, has already paid me once for this stuff, and now you are paying me again for much of the very same stuff.

But please understand: It is the mission of every writer to get paid as many times as possible for the same piece of writing.

I learned this lesson from one of the best in the business: Ray Bradbury, author of *Fahrenheit 451*. I was travel editor of *AARP the Magazine* at the time, and I'd heard that Bradbury was a great friend of Walt Disney and a huge fan of Disneyland. So I wrote to him, asking if he would compose a short piece about how Walt came to launch his Fantasyland in Anaheim.

Within a week, I heard back.

"I can write that article with two hands tied behind me and typing with my nose!" Bradbury wrote. "I'll have the article back to you some time during the next two weeks."

We negotiated a fair price, Ray faxed me a signed contract (which I still treasure), and I sat back and awaited the story, anticipating a small masterpiece from a living legend.

True to his word, in a week and a half the article arrived, alive with anecdotes about how Bradbury was dragged to Disneyland by his friend Charles Laughton...how he became so enamored he begged Walt to let him help develop Tomorrowland...and how Walt turned him down, saying, "You're a genius and I'm a genius! We'll kill each other the second week!"

A few months later I was browsing at Barnes and Noble when I picked up a new collection of Ray Bradbury short essays — and to my considerable surprise there was the Disney piece he "wrote" for me, virtually word for word, reprinted from another magazine!

Now, you might expect me to have been upset, or even angry. But no, I was delighted — thrilled even.

If a high-profile writer like Ray Bradbury could get away with shamelessly recycling his stories, I reasoned, just imagine how much stuff a nobody like me could sling around without anyone noticing!

To be fair to myself, many of the pieces in this volume are somewhat longer than their original form — not padded, mind you, but as I like to say, "enhanced." And I've added a couple of pieces I wrote for my dear friends at the Rehoboth Beach Writers Guild, including one of the relatively few pieces of fiction I've ever composed, a story about a pilot who finds himself gliding in a disabled small plane over the towns and farms of coastal Sussex County ("Write what you know," they say, to which I say "Yes, in retrospect you're probably right").

I'm going to mention Terry Plowman for a second time in this foreword because I owe him a debt of gratitude. When my wife Carolyn and I moved to Lewes in 2013, it was my expectation that I would simply use this locale as a new home base for my far-flung writing career, which has taken me all over this country, throughout Europe, to the Middle East, to China and the South Pacific.

Then, one day, Terry wrote to me out of the blue asking if I might be interested in writing a series of articles for *Delaware Beach Life* from the perspective of a new transplant who finds fascination in every new acquaintance, discovery around every turn. That has given rise to a number of feature stories along with two regular columns, "Treasure Hunting" and "Three Questions," that have won some awards and gained a certain amount of local recognition.

I think this collection comprises some of the best writing I've done. In fact, I do believe I'll be able to write the sequel with two hands behind me and typing with my nose.

ALL THE RIGHT WRONG TURNS

Seeking Mates, Vultures Just Wing It

VULTURE CULTURE

What I *wanted* to see was an eagle.

In the months after I moved to Lewes from Washington, D.C., all I heard about from my new hiking, biking and kayaking friends was that glorious moment when the blue sky is split by the sweeping lines of an American bald eagle. From the heavens it swoops, skimming the water, snagging a wriggling fish and zooming skyward again, like a stealth fighter doing touch-and-goes.

Alas, such a spectacle has eluded me. My first close encounter was decidedly unsatisfactory, along Route 50 one afternoon, where on the shoulder an eagle was pecking frantically at a flattened possum. We made brief eye contact. Frankly, I think we were both embarrassed.

Then one morning I stepped out my front door and was startled by the shadow of a great bird flitting across my lawn. I looked up, shielding the sun with my hand, and released an exultant gasp at the sight of the magnificent creature, silhouetted against the sky. Lazily it followed an arc to the north, then circled back.

"What a majestic creation," I whispered to myself as it descended toward me.

"Hmm. It looks like it's missing some wing feathers...

"Wait...why is its head all red?

"My God — WHAT IS THAT HIDEOUS THING???"

With that, a turkey vulture, as far removed from an American bald eagle as a cockroach is from a monarch butterfly, plopped itself down on the street. The thing took a few awkward hops, then used its gnarly beak to flip the carcass of a toad that had apparently failed to elude my tires as I pulled into the driveway the previous night.

The bird's distracted disassembly of the unfortunate toad gave me a chance to get a good look at him (or her; I'm no ornithologist). Its feathers, so striking when seen from below, seemed tattered and worn, like the boa on a down-on-her-luck Copa girl. Its ungainly feet supported a pair of fat legs that resembled Big Bird's, only instead of plush and orange they were raw and red. And that head: A red E.T.-like noggin with scraggly hair-like feathers; dark eyes ringed by fleshy, blood-red concentric circles; and a beak, seemingly stuck on with Krazy Glue, that curls into a nasty hook perfectly contoured for easy removal of intestines and eyeballs.

Of course, turkey vultures may *seem* disgusting and repulsive when you first see them, but the more you get to know about turkey vultures, the more disgusting and repulsive they become. They keep their legs cool by peeing and pooping on them. Their nostrils aren't separated by a septum, so when you see a turkey vulture in profile, you can look right through its beak. When threatened, these birds defend themselves by vomiting partially digested meat, which smells so awful their attackers run off, presumably looking for a bucket to puke in. Turkey vultures can also spew stinging, blinding vomit into their attacker's eyes, just like that dinosaur did to poor Newman in "Jurassic Park."

Why, you may ask, can't turkey vultures be more like their genteel winter companions, snow geese? I mean, just look at those strikingly graceful birds: laying feathery blankets on coastal Delaware farm fields, rising in glorious clouds of white, their voices a chorus of avian music. Turkey vultures can't even sing. They mostly hiss. Sometimes they grunt.

The world could use more snow geese and fewer turkey vultures. Right? Uh, no. Not right. In fact, if not for those turkey vultures patrolling on high, keeping an eye out for dead and dying critters to consume, you and I would be up to our gizzards in dead deer, rancid raccoons, and putrefying possums.

That's what I learned when I caught up with Jacque Williamson, who's not only curator of education at Wilmington's Brandywine Zoo, but also one of the world's top experts on vultures. She was on maternity leave, but her boss gave me her cellphone number because, as he put it, "she is always eager to talk vultures."

He's not wrong about that. Williamson doesn't just like vultures; she lives and breathes vultures, and immediately jumped to their defense.

"They're amazing!" Williamson insisted. "I have a pretty strong passion for vultures."

Mostly, she said, vultures suffer from terrible PR: "Vultures have a bad reputation. They're called the undertakers of the dead. They're associated with death and disease."

That makes sense, since just about the only time we see vultures on the ground is when they've got their ugly little heads buried in some unfortunate animal's abdominal cavity.

A vulture can smell a rotting corpse from 10 miles away, Williamson said, and as it homes in on that tasty treat, other vultures take note and follow. It's a good thing, because if we depended on guys in trucks to carry off all the carcasses vultures eat, the cost would climb into the millions of dollars each year. In fact, Williams calculates, each and every vulture performs the equivalent of hundreds of thousands of dollars in disposal services.

"It's incredible," she enthused. "A wake of vultures can devour an entire large animal in a matter of minutes!"

Wait a minute. A *wake* of vultures?

"Yes!" she said excitedly. "Vultures have the best collective nouns! A group of vultures roosting in a tree is called a committee. When you see them flying in a circle overhead, that's a kettle of vultures. And when they gather around a carcass, that's a wake."

But it would be our funeral if vultures flew the coop, she added. Because vultures have battery acid-like chemicals in their stomachs, their guts destroy the things that might have killed an animal in the first place, like the rabies virus or anthrax bacteria. On the other hand, a fox that takes a bite of a rabies-carrying carcass can catch the disease and spread it.

Still prefer a field covered in snow geese? You should know that your average snow goose is an eating and pooping machine, devouring vegetation — often the young stems of a farmer's spring crop — up to seven hours a day and defecating up to 15 times an hour. And there are more than a million of those guys, eating and pooping like there's no tomorrow.

No wonder hunters are encouraged to shoot up to 25 a day...while bagging a single vulture can get you a six-month jail sentence.

Just try explaining *that* to the guys in the prison yard.

Al Fasnacht On Duty

THE DISNEY NEXT DOOR

A mercifully cool onshore breeze wafted off Rehoboth Beach and filtered through the bustling arcade of Funland.

The mid-August sun had already set behind the boardwalk shops and hotels, and it seemed like everyone who'd been sweating and sunning on the sand that day was now crowding into the mom and pop amusement park. Determined teen boys desperately tried to impress their girlfriends at Super Shot basketball. Families patiently waited their turns at the carousel. Nervous young parents strapped their toddlers into the round-and-round fire engines, perhaps experiencing for the first time the anxiety of watching their little ones do something without them.

For my grandkids and me, the day was coming to an end. We trudged along Delaware Avenue, our flip-flops slapping against the soles of our feet as the music and merriment of Funland faded in the thickening night air.

I felt a tug on my hand.

"Papa," my 5-year-old grandson said, "can we come back to Disney again sometime?"

Al Fasnacht laughs out loud when I tell him that story.

"Disney!" Funland's 91-year-old founder smiles. "That's rarefied company to be in!"

He thinks for a moment.

"But you know, I *get* it."

There is, in fact, a common thread that joins small-town folks like Al Fasnacht with global titans like Walt Disney: a desire, bordering on fanaticism, to share a particular vision — and confidence that the world at large will invest its time and money to experience it. The only real difference among them is scale.

Tourist regions like lower Delaware, where visitors are always looking for something new, are especially fertile grounds for such visionaries. As I sat down with three very different next-door Disneys — an amusement park owner, a campground operator, and a folk artist — it quickly became clear that they see the world a little differently from the rest of us.

They also make that world just a little bit richer.

Al Fasnacht: Along for the Rides

It was the helicopter ride that first got his attention.

Al Fasnacht and his family, who owned a little picnic park near Harrisburg, Pa., were on vacation in Rehoboth in 1962. They dropped in on what was then known as Sports Center — a handful of boardwalk rides and games owned since the 1930s by the Dentino family. Fasnacht, then in his mid-30s, was intrigued with the way the copter ride allowed even a child to control its movements. He fell into conversation with the owner.

"Almost before we said anything else," he recalls, "Mr. Dentino asked me if I'd be interested in buying the place. I said,

'Well, I already have one headache; I'm not sure I need another one.'"

As it turned out, he did: By the following summer, the renamed Funland was being run by Fasnacht, his brother and their parents. Today the park is still under family ownership — five generations of Fasnachts have trod Funland's pavement — with the gray-haired, bespectacled, and still-spry Al on the job every day from opening to closing.

Peer through the fence at Funland each morning and you'll see him patrolling the grounds, cleaning up trash from the previous day. After dark, he heads out to the park's oldest attractions — the kiddie rides — lifting excited kids on and off the boats, fire engines, and Skyfighter rocket ships.

Unbelievably, those three rides have been in Funland even longer than Fasnacht has.

"Just last year a gentleman told me he rode the fire engines 70 years ago!" he says, eyes wide with amazement.

I later did a little back-of-the-envelope math and figured that over seven decades each of those fire engines has traveled more than 160,000 miles — nearly three-quarters the distance to the moon. They even travel in the off-season, when the family hauls them back home to Harrisburg, where they are refurbished.

"Those fire engines couldn't have looked any better when they were new than they do now," Fasnacht says with obvious satisfaction. He's also proud of Funland's crown jewel: The Haunted Mansion, open since 1981. Running only at night — to ensure no daylight seeps in to ruin the effects — the ride lifts guests to a dark, family-friendly scary space above the park's vintage bumper cars.

Funland's Haunted Mansion is no cheap carny attraction: For 10 years, the worldwide Darkride and Funhouse Enthusiasts club conducted a poll to determine America's best haunted house attractions. Every time, Funland's Haunted Mansion finished in the top 10 — and in 2006 it landed in second place, ahead of those other Haunted Mansions in Anaheim and Orlando.

"That's quite an honor," says Fasnacht. "All those huge conglomerates running their amusement parks, and here's little dinky Funland in lower, slower Delaware!

"From the start, I didn't want one of those haunted houses where guys are chasing you with chain saws. I wanted something for the family; something to entertain and amuse.

"I love loading guests at the Mansion. A couple of years ago this lady had a little guy, 4 or 5, who did *not* want to go. He was holding onto the fence, begging her to turn back. She literally dragged him on.

"When they came back around, the kid had this big smile on his face. I asked his mom how he handled it, and she said, 'I don't know — I had my eyes closed the whole time.'

"An hour later that little twerp was back in line with another family member!"

It's 8:30 p.m. and Al Fasnacht is in his element. He's standing by the rotating Skyfighter ride, hand at the ready to hit the big red emergency stop button if one of his young charges should start to climb out prematurely.

One little girl, ignoring the frenzied waves from her cheering parents, has eyes only for Fasnacht. Each time around, she smiles broadly, reaching her right hand toward him as she sweeps past. And each time around, he returns that smile, nodding encouragement as she soars through what, for a 3-year-old, is the adventure of a lifetime.

"This is the best time of my day," he tells me without removing his eyes from the ride (one of the first things Funland operators learn is to never get distracted by conversation).

"People just seem to get special enjoyment out of watching their kids, their grandkids, their great-grandkids on the same rides they enjoyed when they were young. And they always seem to make a special effort to tell us how much it means to them that we're still here.

"My friends back in Harrisburg always tell me I should stay up there and just let the kids run Funland. I tell them, 'You don't understand. The kids *are* running the business.'"

For one moment, Al Fasnacht shifts his gaze from the Skyfighters and looks me in the eye.

"Funland doesn't need me," he says. "I need Funland."

Kenny Hopkins: The Great Outdoors

"There's a BEAR in the campground!"

Kenny Hopkins has gotten a lot of urgent phone calls in the 33 years he's been running Holly Lake campground near Long Neck, and as he listened to the frenzied voice on the line, he knew two things:

One: He had to get out there to investigate, and

Two: "That wasn't no bear."

There's been just one bear sighting in Delaware since Colonial times — although, admittedly, it was in 2018 in Newark. But that night Hopkins dutifully patrolled Holly Lake's 1,000 campsites and finally came up with the likely culprit: a big, black Labrador.

Hopkins wasn't upset, though. The mere fact that one of his campers thought an honest-to-goodness bear might come ambling past his tent flaps confirmed that Holly Lake is everything he wants it to be.

"This is just an old-fashioned campground, the kind you used to go to with your family when you were a kid," he says. "Inside our gate you leave the hustle and bustle of the city. You'll see wildlife: deer in the daytime, raccoons at night, and the ants will try to take your food.

"And while you definitely won't see a bear, you can imagine you might.

"We've got dirt roads, dirt lots, and leaves all over the place from all these trees. It feels like you're really going camping.

"Other campgrounds clear-cut the trees, pave the roads, and have concrete pads. But then you might as well just go camping in the Walmart parking lot."

We're sitting in Holly Lake's Country Campstore and Restaurant. It's a converted old barn, brought to this site by Hopkins' father-in-law 55 years ago. When Holly Lake opened back then, it went without saying the locale was too far out in the country to ever become hemmed in by development. Today this length of Route 24 is bristling with strip malls, gas stations, and sprawling communities — but for a blessed few hundred yards, where a canopy of trees still leans over the road, the low-slung red roof of Holly Lake's slightly ramshackle store beckons irresistibly, as if from another era.

The story of Holly Lake entwines two longtime area families: Kenny Hopkins is of the Hopkins Dairy clan; his father-in-law, Bob Raley, was a pioneering local land developer and co-founder of Nassau Valley Vineyards in Lewes, Delaware's first commercial winery.

When Kenny married Raley's daughter Suzette 35 years ago, he got into the camping game by default. But he took to the new gig like Holly Lake's wood ducks take to the marshy ponds that dot the campground. In the face of encroaching development and a culture that values FaceTime over actual face time, Hopkins toils year-round to create an authentic wilderness experience every summer.

And it's not just for his campers. Take the petting zoo — an old-timey roadside attraction located just behind the camp store, hard against Holly Lake Road. A small gravel parking lot invites passers-by to pull over and run their fingers through the coats of the dozen or so goats that dash to the fence for attention. Buy some animal feed from one of the dispensers and you can become a goat's best friend; the critters practically climb over the barrier to get at you.

Wander around the perimeter of the fence and you'll encounter chickens, pigs, white-tailed deer — and a small herd of animals with short legs, squat bodies and twisting antlers that all but scream "reindeer."

"They're actually fallow deer," says Hopkins. "Everybody thinks they're reindeer. In fact, my mother-in-law got them for my father-in-law for Christmas."

I am in Hopkins' pickup truck, bouncing along Holly Lake's unpaved roads. We pass 30 log cabins he's put in during the past few years, and drive by the concrete pad where in a few weeks he'll be erecting a teepee, just to see how visitors like it. Each camping area is identified by a hand-carved wooden sign bearing the relief image of a woodland creature: raccoon, owl, duck, and so on.

Besides the simple but insistent demands of campground maintenance — two years ago he hauled 1,000 tons of composted leaves off the property — for Hopkins the most difficult balance is in keeping up with modern vacationers' demands while maintaining Holly Lake's timeless, rustic appeal.

"Everyone wants WiFi," he says with a hint of exasperation. "It's the first question people ask us. So we had a company out of Texas put up 52 towers, each with a 300-foot signal radius."

He draws the line at cable TV, though.

"The cable company wants $250,000 a year to put cable in," he says. "If I'm gonna spend that kind of money on something, it's not gonna be cable!"

Holly Lake's 100,000-gallon swimming pool is a recent addition, surrounded by a stockade fence meant to resemble Fort Apache. It's a popular party spot, and although he's not required to by law, Hopkins keeps lifeguards on duty at all times.

"Hiring them is such a pain in the neck," he notes. "If you hire a girl, all the teen boys hang out next to her all day, distracting her. If you hire a boy, he wants to flirt with all the girls all day. If you hire one of each, soon they're dating and if one takes off you lose both of them. Such a headache." But he laughs, so I figure to him it's worth the trouble.

We swing around back toward the country store, once more passing the zoo. Admiring a grouping of those fallow deer, huddled near a shelter, I mention how much my grandkids would love to see them.

"They're also good eating," he adds. Sometimes the farm boy has to assert himself.

Judy and Lou Hagen: Pipe Dreams
The first thing you notice is the life-size giraffes. Or maybe the enormous swordfish, thrashing away in a life-or-death battle with a poker-faced fisherman. Then again, it's hard not to

notice the mermaid, fairly bursting out of her flimsy bikini top as she lounges provocatively on a park bench.

Aw, heck, forget them: The real showstopper is that 20-foot-long flying dragon, threatening to breathe fire on the cars zipping by along John J Williams Highway in Millsboro.

You know that scene in "The Wizard of Oz" where Dorothy exits her black-and-white farmhouse and steps into a kaleidoscopic world of oversized flowers and weird Technicolor characters?

That's sort of what it's like to pull into the driveway of Judy and Lou Hagen. For nearly two decades, their fanciful (and, frankly, slightly twisted) metal sculptures have loomed over passing motorists, inviting one and all to stop by and see what else is lurking behind the couple's house.

As the tires of my car crunch down the gravel drive, it's clear I'm not in Kansas anymore. Up ahead I spot a wildly colorful batch of three-foot-long dragonflies. Looking a little closer, I notice their big round eyes are actually painted ball bearings. And their tails are bent drill bits. And their legs are the tines of old rakes.

There are birds made from car bumpers. Some flowers are fashioned from tilling rotors. Others have garden spade petals. Here and there stand squat little turtles made from military helmets.

But mostly there's Judy Hagen, her blue eyes flashing from beneath a crown of silver hair, her small frame seemingly weighed down by a heavy, well-worn denim jacket.

I find Judy emerging from her shop out back. It's there that she and Lou have for 19 years sanded, shaped, welded and painted fanciful sculptures made from the mountain of metal they've found at flea markets, yanked from yard sales and acquired at auctions.

She sits to chat in the doorway to what passes for a showroom — actually a two-car garage. Lou walks by, gives me a friendly smile and shakes my hand. But he moves on immediately. Lou, Judy explains, doesn't like to be interviewed.

"Lou doesn't play well with others," Judy laughs. "He's more of a man of action."

Married at 18, Lou and Judy, now both 69, spent 30 years in the long-distance trucking business.

"When you own your own truck, you'd better know how to repair it," she says. "So Lou took welding classes, and he became a good welder."

Judy Hagen and Friends

She doesn't really know when she and Lou began adapting their practical skills into artistic ones, but around 2000 they found themselves creating a life-size dinosaur from spare metal parts and setting him up out by the road.

"We called him Dino," says Judy. "Then we made the giraffes, Norma and Lola. And Big Al the fisherman, and Puff the dragon."

As we sit there in the open garage, a large SUV comes rolling up the U-shaped driveway, which loops between the Hagens' house and their gallery/workshop. The driver slows and peers out from behind the tinted windows, but does not stop.

"That's a drive-by," says Judy. "Happens all the time. People see the sculptures out on the street and they just can't resist. They've *got* to see what's back here!"

From the start, the enormous metal figures made a great advertising gimmick — but the Hagens weren't selling anything. Not yet, anyway.

"We never intended this to be a business," Judy says. "We were just having fun. Actually, I just wanted to make some Christmas presents."

But give away enough ingeniously artistic Christmas presents and pretty soon you're creating a demand for your work. And if you're really, really good, the art world just might come calling: The Hagens have two sculptures at Baltimore's prestigious American Visionary Art Museum, which specializes in the creations of outstanding untrained artists.

One of them, a leather-clad woman on a motorcycle, does a wheelie just above the museum entrance. Judy called her Dolly, and it's clear she misses her.

"She's technically on loan," she says, "but how can I take her back?"

Judy is giving me an impromptu tour of the grounds — open to anyone who happens to answer the siren song of her street sculptures. I admire a life-size mermaid figurehead, her torso made from what looks like a cylindrical propane tank, her ample naked breasts created from two old-school oil-filled construction torches. She spits an arc of water into a pool. Above, two whimsical fish-like sculptures, their scales and bones adapted from bicycle parts, among other things, pivot with the wind.

As if she knows what I'm thinking, Judy offers an explanation.

"My brain is wired different," she says, almost apologetically. "Don't ask me to sit down and read a book — but I'll look at a car bumper and see a bird."

Who can count the visionaries in coastal Delaware? The mini golf course owner, the sand sculptor, the museum curator, the boutique brew master... each has a story to tell, a vision to share, and the profound hope that they are not alone in the certitude that their passion is of transcendent value to others.

One more thing the amusement park owner, the outdoorsman and the folk artist have in common: Their passions all came out of nowhere and took them each by surprise.

For the rest of us, that raises a banner of hope: Perhaps we can all be visionaries, if only we keep our eyes open.

High Concept Housing

HOUSE OF FUTURE PAST

My car happens to have a directionally challenged — yet disturbingly assertive — GPS system. Sure, Siri talks a good game, but there are more than a few back-road Sussex County shortcuts that she actively resists for no good reason.

Take Hudson Road. Whenever I leave Route 1 and turn west on Hudson — bypassing Rehoboth while heading to my home near Long Neck — Siri starts barking directions like an O'Hare flight controller. Mostly, she wants me to make a left on Eagle Crest Road, back to her Route 1 comfort zone.

One recent day when I had some time to kill, I decided to let Siri have it her way. Reluctantly, I turned my Honda Civic left onto Eagle Crest and headed back east — past a stately horse farm, past the rustic and charming Burton Chapel AME Church, past the flying saucer...wait, *what?*

I pulled over. Without stopping the engine, I jumped out of the car, leaving the door open, and beelined across the street. The Honda beeped angrily, warning that I was embarking on an unauthorized extra-vehicular activity. "Proceed to the route," Siri nagged.

"Shut up, Siri," I said.

Straddling an expanse of grass, crouching on slender legs, the silvery white form of an honest-to-goodness flying saucer glimmered in the afternoon sun. Not one of those latter-day, post-"Star Wars" iterations with all the vents and gun ports and external engines. No, this was a classic 1950s-vintage saucer, smooth and clean, resembling an egg laid by Godzilla. Large oval windows circled its outer edges.

Best of all, descending from one side was a fold-out stairway. I crouched to see the stairwell disappear into the ship's darkened interior, half-expecting the alien Klaatu and his robot Gort to descend, just as they did in "The Day the Earth Stood Still."

"*Gort!*" I muttered. "*Klaatu barada nikto!*"

The grumble of a small plane engine arose behind me. I turned just as a Cessna cleared some power lines on final approach to a grassy runway that extended beyond the UFO landing site. The lettering on the roof of a large building to my right reminded me precisely where I was: Eagle Crest Aerodrome, a longtime family-owned landmark, harbor to a small fleet of private planes...and, as it turned out, the location of one of the world's few remaining Futuro homes, a revolutionary concept in prefab housing that launched with great fanfare in 1968, then wobbled erratically and crashed spectacularly in the early 1970s.

Of course, I needed to get in there.

Julie Hudson pulls a yellowed poster from a file cabinet. "The Futuro Home," the large type exclaims. Above that is a photo of a saucer-shaped structure that has seemingly come to rest on a roadside.

"It Can Be Purchased Ready To Occupy," the text continues. "Come-See the House Of The Future."

In fact, the saucer in that photo is the very same Futuro house that now sits just a few hundred yards away from us.

"It was the model home," Hudson says. "They had it on display at Five Points, just about where the Coastal Club lighthouse is now.

"It was a good location. You couldn't miss it."

We're in the converted barn, at the corner of Route 1 and Eagle Crest, that now serves as headquarters for Hudson Management. Today the Hudson family owns numerous area properties and businesses, along with Eagle Crest Aerodrome and the adjacent Hudson Fields entertainment venue. It all started thanks to the entrepreneurial spirit of family patriarch Joe Hudson, who began as a farmer, expanded into aviation and then real estate. Along the way, in the early 1970s, he became the exclusive distributor of Futuro houses in five states, including Delaware.

Married to Joe's grandson Christian, Julie runs the day-to-day operations of Eagle Crest Aerodrome, and that includes maintenance of the Futuro house.

"That's my baby," says the mother of four.

The first Futuro house — now sitting in an art museum in Finland — was designed in 1965 by a Finnish architect named Matti Suuronen. Easily transported in 16 pieces and measuring just 26 feet in diameter and 13 feet high, Futuro was was originally designed as a ski chalet. But because it was adaptable to just about any kind of topography — there was even a version that floated on water — backers also saw opportunities to market it as a beach house or vacation home.

Plus, Futuro was seen as the future of affordable housing: It was constructed almost entirely of fiberglass and polyurethane, both made with super-cheap (at the time) petroleum. When they went on the market in 1968, new Futuro houses went for roughly $15,000.

At first it looked like Joe Hudson had hit it big — the Five Points model home was jammed daily, and he had upwards of 17 orders.

But the company's Atlantic City factory was backlogged, and Hudson had delivered only three or four homes before the early '70s Arab oil embargo dealt the death blow: fiberglass and polyurethane prices skyrocketed.

Besides the economic challenges, it turned out not everyone was thrilled with the idea of a spaceship in their neighborhood. Towns began to ban Futuro houses. When Joe Hudson sold one to a guy in Georgia, the state wouldn't allow the thing across the border.

Soon the awful truth was clear: There was no future for Futuro. The company went bankrupt, and the house went the way of go-go boots and fallout shelters.

The former Five Points Futuro spent years at Hudson's housing development, Cave Colony, on Cave Neck Road. Sometime around 1985 it was hauled to Eagle Crest, where it has been turning heads ever since. At times it was used as a family guest house, for a while it was an office, and for many years the Hudsons rented it out to a Chicago man named Richard Garrett, who stayed there when he was in town on business.

"He loved the house," says Julie Hudson, "especially when it rained. He said it sounded like ducks on the roof."

Now the house is vacant, but the Hudsons have plans for its future.

"Let me get the keys to the spaceship," says Hudson.

As we walk across the aerodrome grass, it's clear the Futuro home needs a facelift. The light, neutral coat of paint is peeling in spots, revealing the original dusty blue color underneath. A couple of the windows have small cracks and holes, possibly from someone taking target practice.

"Right now it's kind of a boring color," Hudson says. "We're looking at repainting it something fun, like really bright green or blue."

As originally designed, Futuro's fold-down stairway was meant to double as the entryway door, but the Hudsons long ago installed a traditional door at the top of the stairs. Hudson turns the key, pushes the door open, and leads me inside.

I am standing inside a Faberge egg. Because this is a house where you calculate floor space by multiplying pi times the radius squared, there is not a right angle in the place. A long window seat traces the arc of the opposite wall, painted bright blue. The oval windows seem to emphasize the unrelenting curviness of the interior. Even a dining table and a low coffee table adopt the contour of the circular walls. Projecting from the ceiling are a few feet of white cylindrical chimney that once vented a now-gone fireplace, located at the center of the house. From that chimney remnant hang several spotlights, pointing at the walls.

Having seen vintage Futuro videos, I can tell that the kitchen is virtually intact from the 1970s, including its robin's-egg blue, three-burner electric stovetop and teal cabinetry.

The bedroom is tinier than the tiniest bedroom closet I've ever seen, with a single bed that, because of the room's pie-shaped dimensions, is wedge shaped, wider at the outside wall. The Hudsons will not find a replacement at Mattress Discounters.

There is a shower in the bath, but the room is barely larger than an airplane restroom.

In short, the Futuro house proves what the designers of Disneyland realized a decade or so after Tomorrowland opened: Nothing screams "outdated and impractical" more loudly than futuristic architecture.

So who would want to live in a Futuro house? Lots of people, it turns out – but they're hard to come by. Barely 100 of the homes were built, and today no more than 60 survive worldwide — many of them wallowing in decrepitude. The Eagle Crest Futuro is actually in quite good shape, and the Hudsons hope to make it more than just a roadside curiosity.

"We're planning to refurbish it and do an Airbnb sort of thing," Hudson says. "So anyone can come and spend a night in a spaceship."

And it won't just be local folks, she adds.

"A couple of years ago we had a lady from Finland who just turned up here. My husband asked, 'Can I help you?' And it turned out she had flown all the way from Europe just to see our Futuro house."

In fact, there's a worldwide network of Futuro enthusiasts who spend a good deal of their time making pilgrimages to far-flung sites, sharing their discoveries online.

For the Hudsons, the trick will be in striking the difficult balance between providing modern comforts and preserving Futuro's classic kitsch. They're currently talking with a Georgetown company that designs private aircraft interiors.

"When you think about it," says Hudson, "it's really just a glorified RV. A really, really cool RV."

The sun is setting behind the Futuro house — one of those glorious, otherworldly lower Delaware sunsets. At that moment I realize where I've seen the structure before: In that indelible scene from "Star Wars," when Luke Skywalker emerges from his domed, rustic Futuro-like house on Tatooine to gaze at a double sunset and dream of his destiny.

I aim the Honda at Eagle Crest Road and flip my right turn signal.

"Turn left," says Siri.

Well, if you insist.

Capt. Vance Makes Another Crossing

THE FERRY CAPTAIN

Here on the bridge of the ferry *New Jersey*, somewhere between the twin capes of Delaware and New Jersey, both coasts are sharply etched against the blue late morning sky.

Dolphins are riding the bow wave. Gulls are winging outside the windows, hoping to snatch a fry or two from the passengers on deck. And the horizon gently rises and falls with each forward surge.

But this is far from the deep blue sea, and after 37 years of ferrying vehicles and passengers on the Cape May-Lewes Ferry, Captain Robert Vance, 59, knows every shoal, channel, and buoy along the 17-mile route.

"People get real excited about the dolphins, but we see them all the time," he says. "We see lots of whales — and lots of kinds of whales: humpback, finback. The last one we saw a few weeks ago was a right whale."

Then Vance reveals a little secret that reminds me the ferry is not the mode of transportation to take if time is of the essence.

"If we spot a whale, and it's near our path, we'll actually follow it for a while; get close to it," he says.

"The passengers love that. And if the whale breaches, well, that's better than taking them to Disneyland. I'll announce a whale sighting to the passengers, and they all rush out to the deck to see.

"There's also a practical purpose to that: It helps to have as many eyes as possible spotting the whales, so we know where they are.

"Besides dolphins, in the last four or five years we've also started seeing more and more seals and brown pelicans, which a few years ago we never saw. The range of those animals seems to be moving northward."

From shore, the many tankers and cargo ships in the channel appear to be in a steady single file. But out here, you can see they're scattered around, as if in an oceanic parking lot.

The number of oil tankers, in particular, can actually help predict the price of fuel in the coming weeks. Vance gestures north, to a grouping of massive tankers sitting at anchor.

"Right there is the anchorage, where ships carrying oil products tie up waiting to be off-loaded," he says. "When a bunch of them are lined up waiting, I know they're holding off unloading, and the price of gas is going to go up. When they're all unloaded and just a couple are still out there, gas gets cheaper."

It's smooth sailing today, but I have at times stood on the Rehoboth Beach Boardwalk and watched with some trepidation as the ferry set out in seas that seemed ready to swallow it up. I'm relieved when Vance assures me the ferry never goes out when there's the slightest chance of truly dangerous weather.

But that wasn't always the case. "There was a time when they wanted the ferries always to be going," he says. "I remember one time when we went out in what must have been 15-foot seas. The winds were blowing from the Northeast around 70 miles per hour and gusting up to 90. It was pretty bad. The water crashed in over the bow, blew out a lot of windows, crushed some cars.

"No one was hurt — and of course, these things won't sink. The water just comes on deck and runs out through the scuppers.

"It just so happened that was the night the Rolling Stones were playing at the Vet in Philadelphia, and I had tickets! For a minute there I was wondering if I'd ever get to see the Stones!

"But ferry operators are more cautious now. If we know the weather's going to be real bad, we just cancel operations."

What's more, if there's a hurricane coming, the Cape May-Lewes Ferry literally gets out of town.

"We head upriver," he says. "A few days ahead of Superstorm Sandy we took the ferries up to Philadelphia and docked near the Walt Whitman Bridge. It happens more often than you might think — every year or so."

Less frequently, the ferry is called upon to conduct an at-sea rescue. "When people are in trouble, we're of course inclined to go help them," Vance says, "but there are problems trying to get people aboard the ferry from sailboats and such.

"In 1990 a cruise ship heading for Philadelphia (the 1,300-passenger *Regent Star*) lost its steering and went aground up the Delaware a mile off Fortescue in New Jersey. They couldn't get the thing off a sand bar, so finally the Coast Guard asked us to come up and offload their passengers.

"We sent the ferry *Delaware* up there and they transferred all the passengers over on a gangplank. Then we brought them down to Lewes, and gave them free food and drinks. I'm sure at that point the cruise line owners were just handing their money over to us saying, 'We don't care what it costs, just show them a good time!'"

Cape May is growing closer, and now's the time when Captain Vance needs to focus on his job. That means it's time for me to leave the bridge.

One more question: Did he ever get to see the Stones?

No need for a 19th Nervous Breakdown: He made it just in time.

Donald Benston With Tree #2

THE TREE IN THE '62 CHEVY

I'm told the reason I get to write this column is I notice things that other people don't. But seriously, it doesn't take a Columbo to be startled by a 20-foot-high tree growing through the passenger seat of a 1962 Chevy Impala.

The eye-catching treehicle is parked right along Roxana Road near Frankford. It's one of those things you drive by, and then you ask yourself, "Did I just see that?" Then you make a hasty u-turn to double-check your memory...and perhaps your sanity.

I have pulled to the side of the busy road and ventured up the short driveway toward the front door. I stumble slightly on the steps as I keep my eyes pinned on the four-wheeled planter to my left.

I knock. No answer. But as I come down the stairs a car pulls into the driveway. Out steps a gentleman who seems utterly unflustered by this stranger at his stoop.

"People stop all the time. Every day," explains Donald Benston, who runs a small auto restoration shop on the property. "They want to take a picture of the tree in the car."

Benston takes me on a guided tour. The car is missing a fender, and two of the four headlights hang loose, like the eyes of a broken doll. The old black paint job has given way to vast swaths of red rust. The convertible roof is long gone, so the interior is virtually bare to the metallic bones. And where the front passenger seat should be, emerging from the ground in four sturdy trunks, is an honest-to-goodness tree.

Naturally, I want to know how long the tree has been sitting here, waiting for a ride. I was unprepared for Benston's answer.

"Actually," he says, "this is the second tree."

Of course, there's a story.

"I've been restoring cars since about 1993," he says. "About 20 years ago, a friend of mine brought this one in. He wanted me to put in two rocker panels and a new floor pan and a new trunk pan."

The friend pulled a big army tarp over the car and said he'd pay for the work piecemeal. Benston installed the trunk pan, but that's where the project stalled.

"He got too busy with a lot of other responsibilities — family health problems, a motel by the beach, a golf course," he says. "It was just something he never got back to."

He points to a scrap of fabric on the rusted engine.

"See there, that's what's left of the tarp. It just rotted away."

But then came Tree Number One, giving new life to an all-but-dead project.

"The first tree got to be as tall as this one," says Benston. "It was one solid trunk."

"One day a guy came in here and saw the car. He called the guy who owns it and said he wanted to buy it. So a member of his family came over and cut the tree down so they could move it.

"But evidently they couldn't get together on the deal. It didn't pan out, so the car stayed here. And the second tree grew in."

Benston has lived here since 1963, in a house he moved to the spot from South Bethany. The wood-frame house, built around 1960, had barely survived the 1962 storm, having been washed off its cinderblock base.

"I bought it for $200 — people had stolen everything out of it but the bath tub. But it restored really nicely."

I step back to take some pictures: Benston standing proudly by what was once the driver's door of a sleek black 1962 Chevy Impala. I'm struck by the contrast between the rusting, neglected hulk and the pristine, lovingly restored house behind it — both built almost exactly the same number of years ago.

And it occurs to me that the margin between preservation and decrepitude is slender indeed.

As I drive away from Donald Benston's place, I realize I've been witnessing reminders of that inescapable truth for as long as I've lived in coastal Delaware. There's the small forest that I've watched growing around — and through — a decomposing school bus at the corner of Kendale and Beaver Dam Roads. I'm willing to bet that even now there are buses of similar vintage hauling church groups to camp, yet here raccoons and foxes fight for the best seats, kicking up small piles of broken glass as they skitter down the aisle.

An Ex-Chicken Coop

Out on Deep Branch Road, east of Georgetown, trees even bigger than Donald Benston's punch through the dark windows of a collapsed chicken house, the corrugated metal wall now sloping at a 45-degree angle to the ground, barely supporting the twisted roof. And all along the back roads, clots of trees smother the shells of small wood or cinderblock houses that once found shelter in their shade.

33

But the ruin-in-progress that intrigues me most sits at the intersection of Avalon and Johnson Roads, about halfway between Georgetown and Hollyville. You can barely see it behind the encroaching forest — largely because the structure itself, a huge single-story wood frame building, is itself green. It looks to me like an abandoned conference hall from when this area was a destination for church groups, but Sussex County's public property and tax records are surprisingly spare regarding its original purpose and age.

A tsunami of ivy pushes up the walls and under the eaves. I can see at least one near-perfectly round hole, a few feet wide, puncturing the pine needle-covered roof. At least one green-shingled wall has collapsed under the weight of overgrowth, but its old white shutters cling in place, the crumbling edifice's last, desperate attempt to preserve some structural dignity.

How old is that decaying corpse of a building? Seventy years? Maybe 80? We can imagine it remained in at least periodic use into the 1960s, maybe much longer than that.

And yet, here it is, nearing total demolition by a relentless wrecking crew of trees, undergrowth, precipitation, animals and insects. It's almost invisible now; in another decade, left to itself, it could virtually disappear.

I drive home silently, watching the new "stick built" neighborhoods of coastal Delaware roll by. The lawns are trimmed, the trees just establishing their roots. I wonder what would happen if one day all our lawnmowers ran out of gas forever; if all those crews of hard-working landscapers suddenly took off to pursue theater careers in New York City; if rising sea levels convinced all of us we'd rather keep our feet dry on higher ground.

I'm beginning to think of that disappearing school bus and the collapsing chicken coop and the vanishing green house not as eyesores, but as essential reminders — as cautionary time clocks.

Aren't those ornamental plants out front waiting to cannibalize our exterior walls, given half a chance? Isn't the wiregrass in our lawns plotting an invasion of our living rooms? Don't the weeds that grow from the cracks in our

The Disappearing School Bus

driveways dream of pushing through the floor pans of our SUVs and growing skyward? And those deer nibbling on our hibiscus — how many years before they would butt down our rotting front doors to feast on the Spanish moss hanging from our kitchen cabinets? Twenty years? Fifty?

From The Peninsula to Belltown, before too long the communities we now call home would become as impenetrable as a lost Mayan civilization — buried for centuries until explorers from some future version of The National Geographic Society came hacking through.

Then they'd examine the ruins and wonder: "Why did these ancient people grow trees in four-wheeled chariots? How odd they must have been."

Julie Ellis-Hall With the Author Before He Lost His Pants

A STATE OF BEE-ING

"You're dressed like a bear."

I am at this moment being addressed by a man wearing a thick, white, long-sleeved fabric top, his face obscured by the netting in a piece of headgear that resembles a CDC containment outfit. In the yard just beyond him, I catch sight of a cloud of bees darting around a wooden hive, tiny rebel X-wing fighters harassing a Death Star. Their buzzing sounds like the whine of a thousand distant drones.

I glance down at my clothing. I'm wearing dark jeans and a black windbreaker.

"Bees hate it when you wear black," he clarifies. "They think you're a bear."

"Well, should I take this off?" I ask.

"I would," he says. "Bees hate bears. They'll go right for your eyes. To blind you."

Now I am tearing off my windbreaker like it's on fire. Of course, underneath I'm wearing a long-sleeved black T-shirt. I now look like a slightly smaller bear.

But my host, Chris Dominic, doesn't panic. He's been raising bees here behind his house in Ocean View for four years, and he knows what to do. He hands me a white protective top similar to his. As I pull it on I'm impressed by its weight and thickness. Two cords tie it closed to prevent bees from crawling up underneath. Finally, I am issued a pair of rubber gloves.

"Now you're safe!" he says excitedly. We approach the hive, where the bees all seem to be humming the same note (roughly B below middle C, musical experts have determined).

Dominic starts pumping smoke from a metal canister containing smoldering pine needles. It's a bee-soothing technique that dates back to ancient Egypt.

"It's best not to get stung," he says, and I wonder who in the world would contest that opinion.

The buzzing intensifies when Dominic lifts the metal lid off the hive's top box. Standing inside, like thick filing cabinet folders, are eight wooden frames crawling with bees. Teeming with bees. Absolutely covered with jostling, gyrating thoroughly agitated bees.

"They're not happy," mutters Dominic. I take a step back.

With a metal tool that resembles a small, shiny crowbar, Dominic pries out one of the frames.

Dominic, a retired data technician from Washington, D.C., has roughly 30,000 bees, all descended from a single queen he had delivered — along with three pounds of drones and females — by UPS. They are Italian bees, which are thought to be more laid-back than many other types. But this bunch is acting like they have been deprived of their afternoon cappuccino.

"Let's see if I can find the queen," he says, and I'm thinking good luck with that — it would be like locating your mother at a sold-out Yankee Stadium.

"There she is!" he says almost instantly. "With the red dot."

Pushing her way through the mob, like the pope in St. Peter's Square, is a bee generally indistinguishable from the rest except for a red dot of model paint placed there by the seller specifically to raise the chances of picking her out from the crowd.

"She's been a great queen," says Dominic. I'm touched by the affection in his voice.

At the bottom of the hive, the entrance resembles the doors to Grand Central Station, with little hairy commuters coming and going, pushing past each other without so much as an "excuse me." Many of those arriving have yellow clumps on their feet, like bright booties: pollen from the many flowers they've visited today, up to three miles distant. They wear those booties from flower to flower, shaking them off each time as they provide essential pollination services to the local flora.

The incoming bees also have abdomens swollen with nectar, sucked from various blossoms. Inside the hive they'll share mouthfuls of the stuff with their fellow worker bees, who'll chew the gummy substance for a half-hour or so before passing it on to another. Eventually this shared gunk becomes honey, which the bees will store in wax honeycomb cells for future hive consumption.

It takes eight bees a lifetime of flying, sucking, and chewing to make just one teaspoon of honey. So it takes a lot of bees to feed a hive — and a lot more than that to make enough honey for us to steal for our morning bagels.

Dominic heads into the kitchen of his bright farmhouse and offers me a taste of homemade honey from a half-empty jar. It's delicious, of course.

His wife, Barb, joins us.

"This is Bill," says Dominic. "He came dressed as a bear."

Barb looks at me sadly. "*Ohhhh*," she says.

On the back porch of her house, Julie Ellis-Hall hands me a set of head-to-toe white beekeeper duds: a screened hood, a heavy top, a pair of fingerless gloves, and a pair of thick white pants.

"It's really best if the bees don't crawl up your leg," she says. More timeless wisdom.

Ellis-Hall, a Lewes real estate agent, is a little bummed out. Just yesterday she found one of her hives had died over the winter. It appears the little guys starved to death — but mysteriously, the hive was full of honey.

"It appears they clustered together during a cold snap and stayed that way — they didn't just walk next door to get their honey," she says, a tinge of remorse in her voice.

"Couldn't the cold have killed them?" I ask as we bounce across her Lewes area lot in a golf cart, heading for two hives she keeps at the far end.

"Nope," she says. "Bees can tolerate down to 20 degrees. No matter how cold it gets outside, all their dancing and wing-beating keeps the hive's inside temperature at a steady 90 degrees.

"Even in the dead of winter, the top of a beehive is warm to the touch."

An eighth-generation Delawarean, Ellis-Hall has been an avid hunter and fisher her whole life. And then she discovered beekeeping.

"I've always thought bees were cool," she says. "Then my sister-in-law in Maryland got them — and I knew I just had to have bees."

She's not alone: The Sussex County Beekeepers, part of a statewide organization, meet every first Tuesday in Georgetown. That's where Ellis-Hall met experienced beekeepers who were more than happy to help her get started.

"Some of these people have 900 hives!" she says.

Now she's in her seventh year keeping bees on her six-acre property along Conley's Chapel Road.

We pull up to two humming hives. She removes the top of one and, using a tool similar to Dominic's, separates the frames, breaking the wax seal created by her bees.

She yanks a frame out — and it's as if she has summoned forth a vast apiary army. There are bees everywhere. I can feel and hear them throwing themselves against my protective gear.

I'm vaguely freaked out, but Ellis-Hall couldn't be happier. Even through the combined two layers of netting on both of our hoods, I can see the smile on her face and the happy glint in her eyes as she roots through her bustling hive.

The bees are visibly restless. Ellis-Hall tries to calm them with puffs of smoke, but the pine needles she's using don't seem to be producing much.

Then I feel it: A pinprick on the second finger of my left hand. I look down and see nothing, but the spreading pain is unmistakable.

"I've been stung!" I say in the manner that 1940s war movie soldiers used to say, "I've been hit!"

Ellis-Hall looks at me. Her blue eyes are expressionless, and her words come out flat.

"You need to get away from here," she says. "They're all over you."

I turn and try to hustle toward the house, which is just a few hundred feet away but seems to be dipping beyond the horizon. It's not exactly like the scene in "The Swarm" where Henry Fonda gets smothered by a cloud of killer bees, but I do see two or three hurling themselves against my face netting — which I now notice has a bee-sized hole down around my mouth.

What's wrong with my feet? I can't seem to get beyond a shuffle. It's literally like that dream where you're trying to escape the monster but your feet won't move.

I look down. The protective white pants Ellis-Hall gave me have fallen down around my ankles. Yes, I have my jeans on, but I still look like a guy lurching around the house looking for toilet paper.

It's horrible. And hilarious. And I'm laughing hysterically, because I know this is probably the funniest thing that Ellis-Hall has ever seen.

"Jump in!" It's Ellis-Hall on her golf cart. And yes, she's laughing out loud. I manage to tumble onto the passenger seat. We roll off to safety.

The bees have lost interest. My finger has already stopped hurting. Ellis-Hall presents me with a little plastic bear filled with honey from her hives, and I feel like a child presented with a lollipop after getting a boo-boo.

I actually think I may have the temperament for beekeeping. But my community doesn't allow beehives, so I'll never know the quiet pleasures (and occasional panics) of this hobby. I keep thinking of Chris Dominic's hives, pressed close up against the back of his house, and the large Adirondack chair that he's positioned just 10 feet or so away from them.

He sits there often.

"How can you not love it?" he asks with a faint smile. "All those little bodies flying around, and that hum.

"*Hummmmmmmmmmm...*"

He's nailed it. B below middle C.

High Steaks

A LOAD OF BULL

Something about tourist towns seems to inspire the oddest of oddball business attractions.

When I lived in L.A., my favorite doughnut shop was in the shape of a giant doughnut. In Florida I entered an alligator farm by walking into the mouth of an enormous 'gator. Atlantic City has the legendary Lucy, a six-story landmark in the shape of an elephant.

For a while I thought coastal Delaware might be an exception. Sure, there's the flying white baby grand piano atop the Keyboard America sign along Coastal Highway. And the retired crop-dusting plane posted above Midway Speedway. And then there's that swooping Huey helicopter behind the fence of Bethany Beach's National Guard training site. (Here's a joke I just made up: Heading north from Bethany you can visit Huey, Dewey, and Louie's Pizza.)

But those things aren't ginormous versions of something — they're totally life-sized. Overall, our neck of the woods seemed to have avoided that traditional tourist trap bigger-is-better mentality.

Then there's Bob the Bull.

You can't miss Bob. He's a roughly 15-foot-high, 20-foot-long black fiberglass bull. If Bob's sheer size won't stop you, his attire will: He's wearing a checkered chef's hat. And a red napkin tied around his massive neck. And sunglasses.

He sure gets my attention — one look at Bob and I veer off Armory Road in Dagsboro, my tires crunching into the pebbled parking lot of the Parsons Farms Produce market. I find myself standing feet from the colossal bull's eye-level snout.

Next to me stands a woman in shorts and a "Mamma Mia!" T-shirt. Even through her dark shades, I can see her eyes were wide in amazement.

"This is the bull from Ocean City, isn't it?" she chirps excitedly. "*Isn't it?*" she repeats, clearly seeking affirmation.

She seems so certain I have to agree. But is it? And if so, how did this super-sized bovine find its way from Ocean City, Md., to a farm store in Dagsboro?

It turns out that move wasn't even the half of it: When it comes to being a traveler, Bob is one well-seasoned hunk of beef. Over the past 40 years or so, he's lived in no less than four states and covered thousands of miles.

I head inside, past the succulent-looking peaches and beyond the shiny apples, and find the owner, Paul Parsons. He's out back, sharing lunch with his wife, Brittany, their baby daughter, Scarlett, and Paul's dad, Preston.

I'm surprised when he informs me that Bob the Bull is a relative newcomer to coastal Delaware: He's been looming over the Parsons parking lot only since spring of 2018. But his presence there was Paul's dream for nearly two decades before that.

"I've wanted Bob here since 2003," he says. "I couldn't get him then, but last year I got a second chance."

Those who ventured south to Ocean City in the mid-1970s will remember Bob the Bull standing at attention outside Capt.

Bob's Steak and Seafood House on 64th Street. He went by the name of Mr. Ocean City in those days, and he became a landmark families waxed nostalgic about all winter long while reflecting on their summer vacations. Generations of parents tracked their kids' growth by how high they measured up to Mr. Ocean City compared to last year's photo.

Besides those countless photos, waves of inebriated college students tried to climb Mr. Ocean City over the years — leading the owner, Bob Wilkerson, to coat it with Vaseline in an effort to discourage them.

Wilkerson bought his big bull from a Wisconsin company that specialized in such things. (FAST Corp. is still in existence, providing playgrounds with whimsical fiberglass slides and high schools with monumental fiberglass mascots. When Mr. Ocean City was delivered from a half-continent away, Wilkerson was surprised to see him roll into town on a flatbed pulled by a station wagon.)

In later years, Wilkerson began to dress Mr. Ocean City in festive holiday costumes: as a bully ghost for Halloween, as Santa Bull for Christmas. Folks in Ocean City couldn't wait to see what that bovine landmark would be wearing next.

Alas, in 2003 Capt. Bob's closed, and the new owners didn't want a big bull in the parking lot (the building is now occupied by Dead Freddies Island Grill, the name of which largely explains why I don't ever go to Ocean City).

It was then that Paul Parsons, hearing the bull was up for sale, got the itch to buy Mr. Ocean City. But the Parsons family was heavily involved in shifting their business from poultry to produce. For reasons hard to fathom, shelling out the money for a two-ton fiberglass bull in a chef's hat just wasn't in the budget.

"We really wanted that bull," says Parsons, still sounding a bit mournful.

So, Mr. Ocean City instead went to a buyer named George Katsetos, owner of Maria's Family Restaurant in Chincoteague, Va. He was renamed Bob the Bull in honor of his original owner — and also because he now lived nowhere near Ocean City. At first, the big fella took a place of honor in front of the restaurant, but then the city got involved, telling Katsetos the thing was just too, well, *big*. Reluctantly, he moved it out back, and the city wasn't too happy about that, either.

Humiliated and unwanted, Bob the Bull fell on hard times. Workers cutting nearby trees let a branch slam into his flank, leaving a gaping hole. Grass grew tall around him. People who'd loved Bob the Bull sought him out, saw the carnage, and left with their heads bowed in sorrow.

But Bob was not ready to be put out to pasture.

The town kept pestering Katsetos to get rid of the bull, and he finally gave in.

By some amazing stroke of luck, Paul Parsons' mother, Cora, saw on Facebook that Bob was once more on the market.

This time the Parsons family didn't flinch. They rushed down to Chincoteague the next day.

"I gave him a price," says Parsons, "and he said, 'You know he's got a hole in him, right?'

"I said, 'Yep!'

"It was a bargain. He just wanted it gone."

On Nov. 1, 2018, Bob the Bull was carted away on a flatbed — and taken straight to Stratoglass Fiberglass in Ocean City, a company that specializes in fiberglass fabrication and repair.

"The strangest thing happened that day," adds Parsons' dad, Preston. "When we pulled into the fiberglass shop, a car pulled in behind me. It was the daughter of the man who used to own Capt. Bob's Steak and Seafood!

"She jumped out of her car and said, 'I'm just so glad someone saved him!'"

It took a winter of work, but by spring of this year, Bob the Bull was ready to roll.

"They did an amazing job," says Paul Parsons. "He was too big to get into their shop, so after they repaired the hole, they actually had to cut another entryway so they could work on him from the inside all winter."

On March 20, Bob was loaded onto another flatbed and gently rolled the 20 miles or so to Dagsboro.

Since then, Bob the Bull has been discovered by the popular Roadside America website, and that's bringing in big-bull seekers from all over.

"I thought they'd be interested in the history of it," says Parsons. "But, no, they just want to see the big bull.

"We want to get back to making costumes for Bob, like they used to down in Ocean City. But there are only so many hours in the day."

I leave the Parsons family to finish their lunch. Back outside, Bob the Bull continues his eternal gaze, peering over the rims of his sunglasses.

"He's had quite a busy life," says Parsons. "We like to say Bob the Bull has retired to the farm."

Marti Garrett Makes Women Happy

THE BRA FITTER

For years, Marti Garrett has been fitting bras at Something Comfortable in Rehoboth Beach — the only certified bra-fitting shop in lower Delmarva.

"Certified?" you may ask. "Is this not just a juvenile excuse to write about an article of clothing that has intrigued, tantalized, and terrified you your entire life?"

Yes, yes it is.

As I was saying, here I am — a guy who since childhood has hustled past the lingerie department like a starving man headed for a steak — surrounded by bras of every imaginable color and style. I've been known to park on the far side of Macy's just to avoid passing through what in less enlightened times was called the Foundations Department.

Now I'm listening intently, or at least trying to, as Garrett explains why there's a lot more to a good bra fit than knowing your cup size. And I can't believe I'm even writing this.

First of all, bra-fitting certification is a real thing.

"There are several bra academies in the U.S. that provide bra-fitting certification," says Garrett as I desperately endeavor not to envision the final exam.

"The course involves a series of up to 18 units — they can be in-person or online.

"A true bra fitting starts out with measurements for the bra band and cup sizes but there's so much more than that. Just because two people are roughly the same size doesn't mean they should wear the same bra.

"Every bra maker is different, even in the same size," she says, and for the first time I'm relating to this: Ask any man who wears size 36 jeans what his *actual* waist measurement is.

"I never knew there were so many different types of bras until I started working here," Garrett continues. "Ours range from 30 AA to 56 J — and actually, cup sizes can go all the way up to 'O.'"

At this point I feel like I need to sit down, but that would involve ducking into one of the dressing rooms.

"We have about 200 types of bras in this shop," Garrett persists, "and we have about 20 of each in different sizes. So that's about 4,000 bras under one roof."

I can't help but scan the walls. Bra after bra, in rank and file, like a bald-headed army on the march.

"You'll find most of them in high-end department stores, I suppose," Garrett says, her words filtering through my personal fog. "But what makes the experience different here is the expertise we bring to fitting a woman with just the right one. The training makes the difference. We have women who drive for two hours to be fitted for a bra here."

My mind snaps to attention. *Two hours?* That's a lot of driving.

"It's almost like women are looking for a good engineer to help them defeat gravity," I offer, somehow putting all this bra talk into a guy's parlance.

"It's true!" she smiles. "First of all, it depends on what kind of job you want your bra to do. Is it strapless? Does it need to be backless? Sometimes you need a plunge, which is almost frontless."

My inner Homer Simpson is whispering, *"Frontlesssss..."*

"The most important thing is to have the bra remain parallel to the floor," says Garrett. "If the strap begins to slip up in back, then the breasts will pull it down even more in the front, and a woman will start hunching over. A properly fitted bra will do wonders for your posture. And your lower back is going to thank you at the end of the day."

For an unguarded moment, I think about the little twinge I've been feeling in my lower back recently. Then I mentally slap myself in the face.

"Often we tell women, 'You've lost 10 pounds with a properly fitted bra because your breasts are off your belly and now you have a waist!'" says Garrett. "I wouldn't want to say definitively, but I suspect there are women who probably should have tried a good bra-fitting before they had breast reduction surgery."

But the best part of being a certified bra specialist, Garrett added, is helping women who've had mastectomies.

"That's especially rewarding," she says. "I can't tell you how wonderful it is to see a woman come in here not happy with herself after surgery — and leave here with a big smile on her face saying, 'I love the way I look.'"

Suddenly my mind is clear. A certified bra specialist isn't just someone who sells underwear: She's also a confidante, psychologist, and physical therapist.

I head back out onto Rehoboth Avenue and look up the street toward Carlton's Men's Wear. I have a sudden urge to buy a tie.

Cape Henlopen Sunset

INTO THE SUNSETS

Entangled in the cables of the Indian River Bridge, the setting sun slips toward the horizon beyond Rehoboth Bay. It's nearly 50 degrees out, but the wind whipping from the Atlantic makes the air feel a lot colder than that. The tidal gush pouring through the inlet from the sea, drawn by the gravity of that sinking orange ball, seems intent on extinguishing its remaining warmth.

No other humans are in sight, so I share this deepening spectacle with a lineup of seagulls. They stand at attention on the jetty rocks, facing down the sun with an intensity they usually reserve for tourists cradling bags of Thrasher's fries.

Along the horizon, a dark line of low clouds shifts to deep purple as the sun dips behind it. Almost imperceptibly, the sky above me morphs to royal blue. Between those cool blankets of color a ribbon of fire flashes from north to south, flaring bright yellow, then dimming to soft red.

For my feathered companions, the show is over. They flap away to wherever seagulls spend the night. But I sense something coming; a curtain call reserved for the patient observer.

And here it is: Above me, a lacy curtain of high clouds explodes in a blush of rosy red that grows to encompass much of the sky. Then, like a supernova expending itself, the crimson stain retreats, and the sky goes dark.

It is night.

If you happen to have a lot of friends in Southern Delaware, you well know that Delawareans tend to obsess about their sunsets. I'm pretty sure Facebook's Mark Zuckerberg has got the actual data lurking someplace, but it's my casual observation that social media sees more per-capita sunset postings from Southern Delaware than just about anywhere else.

I'm guilty of this myself. It's not like we need to pull out easels and oil paints to capture sunsets, Joseph Turner-like — our pallets are in our pockets, and besides that the iPhone has a sneaky way of making a sunset's reds that much redder and its clouds that much swirlier. A touch of the screen and that glorious image is delivered into the hands of all our friends (as well as our "friends"), along with a breathless account to the effect that "Delaware has the BEST SUNSETS ANYWHERE!!!"

Our more far-flung acquaintances, bless their little hearts, respond with pale, washed-out sunset images of their own. We acknowledge them with generous "likes" and "loves," but privately we shake our heads, pitying those whose sunsets fade in a dull Fuji Film snapshot while we bask in the widescreen glory of nightly Super Panavision Technicolor.

It's a safe bet that Dave Green has watched more Delaware sunsets on purpose than just about anyone. It's his job, in a way: In season, he welcomes visitors aboard his boat *Discovery* in Lewes, then noses the craft along the Lewes-Rehoboth Canal and either up the Broadkill River or out into Delaware Bay. These excursions have one singular intention: To give Green's passengers a front-row seat to that fiery ball snuffing itself out on the horizon.

Green, whose day job is in real estate, didn't originally set sail to be a sunset impresario. His dream was — and still is —

to provide scheduled water taxi service between Lewes, Rehoboth Beach, and Dewey. But when plans for a dock in Rehoboth fell through in 2012, Green had to find another use for his boat. The answer to his dilemma was, in the words of Horace Greeley, to "Go West, young man!"

"One evening," he recalls, "my wife and kids and a buddy of mine sailed up the Broadkill, and then came that sunset.

"Once you get past civilization on the Broadkill, you round that corner and you've got the Great Marsh on your left and the Prime Hook Preserve on your right. And the tree line is way, *way* back there. From an inland perspective, it's about the best view you can get of a sunset.

"I said, 'Holy crap, no one knows this is here!'"

For a couple of years, Green stuck to the river for sunset tours; now most of his trips head through the Roosevelt Inlet toward the East End Lighthouse, built in 1885 and silhouetting sunsets ever since.

"We just head out there and start doing doughnuts so everyone gets their picture of the sunset," said Green, who this year has permission to tie up at the end of the breakwater and usher his passengers ashore

"People are just in awe of the sunsets. They go bonkers. My favorite comment ever was from a 5-year-old boy. He just stared at the sunset and said, 'This is the best day of my life!'"

Green has to stay at the wheel, of course, but he admits to sneaking a good long look each trip.

"I've always been a sunset guy," he confessed. "My wife said, 'Oh, you're gonna get so bored just doing sunset cruises.'

"But here's the thing about sunsets: They're like snowflakes. No two are alike."

The cars slow down as they near the spot where I've pulled over on Beaver Dam Road, right where it intersects with Dairy Farm Road.

No one stops, yet I am not alone as I soak in this sunset. A chorus line of cows, lowing softly, is pressed up against a wire fence, facing the reddening sky. Their big bovine eyes and metal ear tags reflect points of twilight.

From this vantage point, tree lines on either side of the vast field before me recede toward the setting sun, adding a third dimension to the tableau. The field's low rills, ploughed into ripples, glow like embers, and at the far end, a mile or so away, the narrow gaps in a tall stand of trees resemble the grates of a glowing fireplace.

The sky purples. The cows raise their heads slightly, then turn and plod toward their evening ritual. I guess it's true: I'll watch sunsets 'til the cows come home.

Southern Delaware folks like to boast that we live smack in the middle of Sunset Central. But do we *really*? It seems almost sacrilegious to broach the question, but couldn't the Delaware Sunset Syndrome be the fruit of the same kind of provincial thinking that causes, say, Californians to claim they have the best skiing and Washington, DC fans to insist they field a professional football team?

I had to admit to myself that maybe, just *maybe*, we in Delaware live under a sunset delusion. But how in the world do you quantify a sunset? How do you grade one area's sunsets against another? To paraphrase those perplexed nuns in *The Sound of Music*, how do you hold a sunbeam in your hand?

Luckily, I've been around long enough to know there's no subject for which there is not at least one expert. And as it happens, there are at least three world-class sunset authorities, and they all work out of Penn State University.

And so today I am driving through the rolling mountains of central Pennsylvania and descending into the comfortable recesses of the place called Happy Valley. There will be no sunset here tonight. Clouds hang low and a cold wind whistles through the campus. I find the entrance to the Walker Science Building, take an elevator to the top floor, and am met by a nice young gentleman named Ben Reppert.

We sit in his small office, crammed with computer terminals and Penn State ephemera. On a coat rack hangs a small selection of neckties, standing by for use during Reppert's nightly appearance on the university's long-running weather program. Like all TV meteorologists, Reppert forecasts rain and fog and wind chill factors. But as a bonus, he's also predicts the quality of each night's sunset.

A 2015 Penn State graduate, Reppert helped hatch the idea for sunset predictions along with classmate and fellow meteorology major Jake DeFlitch, who worked part-time as a university photographer.

"I'd drive Jake around to take pictures, because I had a car," says Reppert. "Many times we'd plan to take a good sunset picture — and it would be a dud. Eventually he came up with this idea: We've got the meteorology education; we can make something that could forecast this. So we thought about it."

Sun Kings: Jake DeFlitch and Ben Reppert

The first question is obvious: What makes a good sunset?

"If you were to ask 10 people how they would define a perfect sunset, you'd probably get nine different answers," Reppert allows. "We decided we wouldn't go for the perfectly clear sky, with no clouds around, no color. We set as our base sunsets where clouds get lit up with the reds and the oranges."

As it turns out, there are just a few, very easily identified, conditions that create that kind of sunset. Reppert pulls out a sheet of paper and sketches a sublimely simple atmospheric cross-section.

He draws a curved line, representing the Earth, with a stick figure (me) at one end and the setting sun at the other — each of us just out of each other's line of sight due to the Earth's curvature. Near the sun he draws the distinctive weather map "H," indicating a high-pressure system with clear skies. At my end he draws an "L", denoting a low-pressure system. Then he adds some clouds — one layer very high up in the atmosphere, the other closer to the ground.

"Ideally, the air near the sun's horizon at sunset is completely clear, with very little water vapor," says Reppert. "As the sun sets, the light passes through the thick, clear, air, which acts as a prism and pulls out the red and orange wavelengths."

But those brilliant colors will simply refract off into space unless there's something to reflect them back to Earth, and that's where those clouds come in.

"I like to think of the clouds as a projection screen," he says. "The clouds catch those reds and oranges. And when they're at different levels they catch different wavelengths of sunlight, so you get that spectrum of colors."

There's more to it, of course, but ideally, a sunset viewer should be standing in a low pressure zone gazing toward a high pressure zone in the direction of the lowering sun.

Armed with their definition of a perfect sunset and their list of ideal weather conditions to create one, Reppert and DeFlitch enlisted an undergraduate computer whiz, Steve Hallett, to work up a program into which they could feed atmospheric data for any given spot — and get reliable predictions for a given evening's sunset quality. The result is a map that displays a color-coded North American continent with hues from cold blue, for minimal sunset beauty, to hot red, the kind of sunset against which you'd expect to see Scarlett O'Hara shouting, "I'll never be hungry again!"

They started a company, SunsetWX, and began posting nightly sunset and sunrise quality predictions on their website (www.sunsetwx.com). No one took much notice until November 22, 2015, when their projection map showed a blood-red gash stretching across one of the nation's most densely populated regions, from Washington DC to Philadelphia, up through New York City and into New England.

"We said, 'We should be Tweeting this!" says Reppert. The prediction was spot-on: *Slate* magazine and *Good Morning America* took notice, and SunsetWX was propelled to success that now includes a partnership with the Weather Channel.

Reppert seems a little hurt when I tell him that sunset skipper David Green isn't really a fan of his service.

"I don't like people trying to cherry pick their sunsets," Green told me, and for obvious reasons: If the forecasters predict a fizzle, folks will be less likely to climb aboard that evening.

"I guess I understand," Reppert says sadly. Then he perks up. "But our forecast only goes out a day or two ahead. People probably make their plans long before that."

Eventually, I have to put the critical question to Reppert: In the Big Book of American Sunsets, just where to Southern Delaware sunsets rate?

He smiles. I feel like he's going to give me good news.

Sunsets happen every evening, and they're difficult to miss, so it's not surprising that people have been ascribing significance to them for most of history.

Even in the Bible, Jesus Himself vouches for the veracity of the apparently *very* old trope, "Red sky at night, sailor's delight" (and if religion is not your thing, Penn State's Ben Reppert concurs).

F. Scott Fitzgerald looked at sunsets as frames of beauty ("Her face, ivory gold against the blurred sunset that strove through the rain…") and also of dread ("The Montana sunset lay between the mountains like a giant bruise from which darkened arteries spread across a poisoned sky").

As for sunsets and me, we go back a long way. Among my earliest memories is sitting on my bed in Dumont, New Jersey, watching the sky turn red over the nearby Safeway supermarket (Hey, when you grow up in North Jersey, you take your Nature's Wonderland moments wherever you can). As a 16-year-old, standing with my brother Ed on a hilltop above Florence, Italy, I caught my breath as the dimming sun set the red tile roofs of Tuscany ablaze — and wished, for a moment, that I was standing there with someone other than my brother Ed. In Sedona, Arizona, I marveled as the sun's bloody rays emulsified with the air's suspension of red dust, creating a sense of swimming through crimson plasma. Some of the world's most dramatic sunsets unfold with your back to the sun: From the summit of Hawaii's Mauna Kea, I watched the volcano's lengthening shadow race eastward across the Pacific, and at Yosemite's Inspiration Point I witnessed purple silhouettes climb the valley's sheer walls.

Sunsets can even have lifelong consequences. In 2010 I was at a convention in Orlando, where I made a dinner date with a female colleague I had only recently met. As dinnertime approached, from my seventh-floor hotel room window I could tell the sun was going to set, spectacularly, over the distant castles and domes of Walt Disney World. I raced down to the lobby and found my dinner companion waiting at the restaurant door.

"This is going to sound crazy," I stumbled, "but the sun is about to set and I'm going to have a terrific view from my window upstairs. Would you mind coming up for just a couple of minutes?"

Well, *that* could have gone any number of ways. But she smiled sweetly and said, "Sure! I love sunsets."

As it turned out, the sunset sort of fizzled. But true to my word, I got us back to the restaurant in time for our reservation. And oh yeah, I married that woman. And I still call her to the window when the western sky goes epic, and she still says, "I love sunsets." She's perfect that way.

Most of us watch sunsets because they're beautiful: In Key West, Florida, and Santorini, Greece, the setting of the sun sparks bacchanals of drinking and dancing. But there are also those who insist sunset watching is somehow physically and mentally good for you. An Indian guru named Hira Ratan Manek claims to have fasted for 15 years — nourished only by sunlight, which he absorbed by looking directly at sunsets and sunrises (Even health guru Dr. Andrew Weil, as wholistic a physician as you'll find, warns that the practice, called sun-gazing, "carries a real risk of retinal damage. I urge you to avoid it"). And *Psychology Today*, noting a study at University of California, Berkeley (where else?), reported that stopping your daily activity to admire a billowing sunset is an instinctual way to disengage, if only for a moment, from fretting about the past and worrying about the future.

Some folks swear by them, but I've always considered sunrises to be the poorly dressed stepsisters of sunsets. And while Penn State's Ben Reppert and his colleagues do indeed issue sunrise quality predictions each day, it's gratifying to hear him affirm my somewhat judgmental attitude.

"Sunsets have a better chance of being spectacular," Reppert says. "During the course of the day the sun heats the ground, so warm air rises, which promotes clouds. Overnight you don't have rising air, so you have a hard time producing clouds in the morning. You have better sunsets mainly due to the fact that you have more clouds to get lit up."

Even Delaware die-hards have to admit that when it comes to consistency in sunset shows, America's Desert Southwest is the reigning heavyweight champ. The desert air is uncannily clear, and when it reflects off the high clouds that typify a dry climate, it's like Monet has been reincarnated as a skywriter.

But there's no shame in a strong runner-up showing: Reppert says that Delawareans are not wrong when they get boastful about the frequent beauty of their sunsets. It has a lot to do with Lower Delaware's distinctive locale: We sit here at the ocean with the broad, flat Delmarva Peninsula spreading to the west. The moist climate of the wide Chesapeake Bay lies beyond that, followed by the whole of North America.

"It's a unique circumstance," he says. "Along America's West Coast, say in California, it's hard to get a good sunset. You've got water going forever to your west. There can often be a lot of clouds over that water, and often they're low.

"In Delaware, though, you have water to the east and water to the west, enough moisture to promote cloud development overhead. But there's also a lot of land to the west, so you have the sun setting over a dry land mass. That's an ideal case — in

Delaware you can bet on having clouds overhead, but the sun is passing through an area that is land-based and clear."

Choke on *that* Malibu!

There's also the matter of South Delaware's expansive sky. The land is flat, of course, but because the area was cultivated as farmland for centuries, there also aren't a lot of big trees to get in the way of our skyscape. As a result, the sun here not only has a full palate of paints, it also boasts a canvas that stretches from horizon to horizon and as high as a circling red tail hawk.

There aren't many places on the U.S. East Coast where you can stand at the lip of the Atlantic and watch the sun set on the horizon. Cape Henlopen happens to be one of them, but from March through August, much of the cape's prime sunset-watching beach is closed to mere humans and instead dotted with nesting red knots, piping clovers, and oystercatchers.

And so for this early spring sunset I find myself on the cape's pier, sharing the plank-and-concrete finger with a dozen or so fishing enthusiasts — that is, if you can define "enthusiast" as one who drops a hook in the water, then leans back in a folding chair, closes his eyes and starts nodding to beats in his earbuds.

The air was comfortably warm when I came out here, but as the sun approaches one diameter of the horizon — marked by a pencil-thin line of trees — a cool breeze from the west has kicked up. I turn my back to the wind. The whitewashed Harbor of Refuge Light House is bathed in pink, slowly shifting to a deeper shade of red, as are the frothy wave tips playing about its base.

Back to the west, the Sun's disk has called it a day. An inbound Cape May-Lewes Ferry, silhouetted against the darkening sky, slips by. A few passengers stand on deck, their cameras flashing in a ridiculous effort to illuminate the cosmos.

I turn to leave, but am stopped in my tracks. Although the sun is gone, all around me the horizon has become a glorious cyclorama, aglow with a ghostly belt of red, translucent against a field of deepening blue.

The sound of the wind and waves seems to fall away. My eyes search the length of the pier. Is anyone else seeing this?

I glance back at the earpod fisherman. He's still nodding. But his eyes are open.

In Delaware, It's Always "Hi" Time

CATCH THE WAVE

At first I was a little weirded out. I'd just moved to Delaware — so how did just about everyone here seem to know me?

It didn't matter if I was walking in my new neighborhood, bicycling along the back roads, or even sitting at intersections in my car. Just about every person I encountered...*waved.*

I waved back, of course, half expecting the interaction to continue. But no — those folks went on about their business. Sometimes I'd notice them waving to the person behind me, too.

Eventually I just started calling this phenomenon The Delaware Wave. I've lived, in order of appearance, in New York City, northern New Jersey, Los Angeles, Palm Beach, Fla., Washington, D.C., and Bethesda, Md. Never in any of those places did I find myself being greeted with such jaunty enthusiasm by complete strangers.

I haven't been able to find any academic or historic explanation for it, but I have a theory that has to do with the unique social dynamic of coastal Delaware: Until very recently — and by that I mean just a few decades ago — the area south of Dover was sparsely populated by farmers, the merchants who served them, and the folks who ran the seasonal beach destinations.

In those days, everyone really did know everyone else, and to refrain from waving when the fellow from the next farm passed by wasn't just bad form, it could lead to resentment (Why didn't Abner wave to me?), gossip-mongering (Abner must have something to hide), or worse (Abner must *die*).

Then came the influx of newcomers, surging into Sussex County like Canada geese, bringing with them just as much noise and almost as much poop. The old-timers kept waving, and the aliens just followed suit.

Of course, varying levels of familiarity developed, leading to endless variations on the old "howdy, neighbor" Delaware Wave. As a public service, here is a primer on these gestures, and what they signify:

The Delawarean

The most common Delaware Wave can best be described as approximating the way Indians used to say "How" in old Hollywood westerns: Arm extended to the side, bent upward to a right angle at the elbow, fingers straight. Occasionally accompanied by a slight parting of the lips in a mimed "Hi."

The Enthusiast

Rarely seen but unmistakable, this Wave resembles the appearance of a frantic third-grader trying to get the teacher's attention, as in "Oooh! Oooh! Call on me!!" Reserved for best friends and sisters who spot each other at opposite ends of the Tanger Outlets parking lot.

The Midway

Usually adopted by guys who think they're cool: arm straight out to the side, palm facing forward, akin to the gesture of a batter who has just hit a home run and is slapping five with the base coach while rounding third. A particularly nonchalant form of the Delaware Wave, this one frequently occurs without eye contact. Adopters of The Midway aren't quite antisocial, but they're not particularly friendly, either. Do not trust them.

The Low Five

The arm is barely raised, the hand bends outward at the wrist, palm facing the ground. Nearly imperceptible finger movement may be present. This form of the Wave is often adopted by recent big-city transplants who are just getting used to this whole Wave thing — especially when they think they recognize the car that's coming, but can't quite make out the face of the person behind the wheel and are not positive it's someone they're comfortable waving to.

The Finger

Not as offensive as it sounds, this is actually a friendly, if minimalist, Wave. The waver smiles and points at the recipient, like a politician singling out random faces in an applauding crowd. This waver is saying, "Hello, you. Yes, I mean *you!*"

The Wiggle

As noncommittal as the Wave can get, this one consists of a mere flutter of the fingers at the end of a floppy arm. It's totally insincere and more of a kiss-off than a greeting. These wavers have retired to Delaware only to realize it's not for them. Soon they will be moving to The Villages in Florida, where they can stay in their air-conditioned houses all day and not wave to anybody.

The Swat

A particularly violent form of the Wave, this variation involves adopting the bent-arm, upright-hand pose of the classic Delawarean, but in this case the hand is forcefully swept downward, as if the waver were crushing a tarantula on an imaginary tabletop. As coastal Delaware's population grows, the Swat is, alas, becoming increasingly common: The waver has been waving all day, and his or her arm is now growing tired. "I'm waving at you, okay?" the waver is saying, with some exasperation. "What more do you want from me?"

The Wheel Grip
You would think the crush of cars in the area would slowly kill off the Delaware Wave, but happily it has actually added to the traditional wave lexicon. Drivers who wish to reciprocate a pedestrian's friendly wave have many options, among them the 10-Finger Palm Wave: While keeping their hands at 10 and 2 o'clock on the wheel, they flare their fingers upward. More cautious drivers will raise one or two fingers in greeting. The most enthusiastic drivers have been known to actually roll down their passenger windows and engage in more traditional, emphatic Delaware Waves. Concerned DelDOT officials are reportedly considering initiating a "Don't Wave and Drive" campaign.

The 'My Bad'
Sadly, we're beginning to live so close to each other in coastal Delaware that interpersonal conflicts are inevitable. That can lead to the uncomfortable moment when you reflexively begin to wave at someone, then realize to your horror that that's the guy whose dog keeps leaving deposits on your lawn. When caught in mid-Wave, the default resolution is to move your hand to your hair, as if flattening down a stray curl. Those without hair up top face a more complicated choice as to where that hand should go, but frankly I'll pick my nose before I wave to *that* guy.

Just the Guy You Want Pestering You

THE PEST MAN

Rick Blauvelt is a little nervous about being interviewed about his work, even though his professional title — associate certified entomologist and vice-President of the Delaware Pest Control Association — is more impressive than any job description I'll ever have.

Still, it's understandable. As technical director for Activ Pest Solutions in Lewes, I'm sure he's sensitive to all the stupid, jokey questions people ask about exterminators and insects: "What bugs you most about your job?"... "Can you get rid of the mouse next to my computer?" ... "Do people think you're a real buzz killer?"

But I've already spent the last 10 minutes talking to myself out in the parking lot, getting those jokes out of my system. Now it's strictly business.

Blauvelt is a smart, affable fellow, just the kind of guy you'd trust injecting deadly chemicals into the ground around your house. After 20 years in the business, he says, there's not much about bugs that bugs him.

First off, I ask him to settle an argument for me: I say ants are pretty clean insects when you compare them to, say, cockroaches.

Immediately, I lose the argument.

"Our number-one call here is for ants," he says. "People tend to see them as a nuisance, but they also carry a myriad of pathogens. They can contaminate your food, your counters.

"The most prevalent ant here is the odorous house ant. It's called that because if you crush it between your fingers it'll smell like rotten coconut. There's also a little black ant that's called the little black ant."

Wow, I'm thinking: The committee in charge of naming ants could really use a creative writer or two. I'd call the odorous house ant the Pumba Ant, after the farting warthog in *The Lion King*. And the Little Black Ants would be Chocolate Jimmies.

The biggest beef I've heard from friends about pest management companies is that they're always bugging you (ha!) to sign up for a service contract. I recall having a house near D.C. protected against termites 25 years or so ago, and the little critters never came back.

But Blauvelt sets me straight: It's a classic case of That Was Then, This Is Now.

"It's true you used to be able to treat once and the pests would never come back again — 20 years later the chemical would still be there killing stuff," he says.

But then those pesky varmints in Washington, D.C. got into the act. For reasons unknown, they took exception to the notion of turning all of our homes into little self-contained Love Canals.

"Take the stinkbug, for instance," he says, invoking an insect name I would definitely leave just the way it is. "There was a time when you could basically paint the side of the house with chemicals that were very good at getting rid of them. But now those options are off the table.

66

"All the materials we use today are designed to break down rapidly in the environment. That's why you need routine inspections and timely treatments."

I've been saving my most critical question for last; a stumper that has gnawed at me ever since an unfortunate incident at my girlfriend's house during my teen years.

"Suppose, just for the heck of it, I had a bat in my house," I ask. "Is it a bad idea to chase it around with a tennis racket?"

My words are still hanging in the air when Blauvelt jumps all over them.

"Yes!" he fairly shouts. "That's a bad idea! Don't do that, ever! Very bad!

"Here's what you do: Turn off all the lights and open the windows. He'll follow a wind current out. Don't worry about other bats flying in. They don't want to be with you any more than you want to be with them.

"But a tennis racket, wow. What you end up with is an injured bat and bat blood all over the place."

I nod solemnly. For a brief moment, our life experiences have merged.

Wood Recognize Him Anywhere

TALL, DARK AND HANDSOME

First of all, Peter Wolf Toth wants you to know it's not a totem pole.

That's not a minor point. For years, whenever I visited friends in Bethany Beach, rather than tell me to turn inland at the intersection of Route 1 and Route 26, they'd say, "Turn at the totem pole."

In fact, I'm guessing that every business on the beach end of Bethany's bustling Garfield Parkway tells customers to "look for the totem pole" when they drive into town. Even Bethany Beach's municipal web page describes the 24-foot-high sculpture as a totem pole.

Uh, nope.

"It's a statue," Toth tells me, and he should know because he's the guy who carved it from a 24-foot-high trunk of western red cedar.

In fact, Bethany's statue, a likeness of the local Nanticoke Indian leader Little Owl, is part of what could be considered one of the most expansive art installations on the planet: The Trail of Whispering Giants. Since 1972, Toth has created a network of more than 74 similarly tall and intricate wooden statues honoring Native Americans — at least one in each state and many throughout Canada

"That statue on the beach in Bethany is a unique one," says Toth. Even over the phone, he seems as excited about it now as he must have been more than 40 years ago.

"If you look very closely, you'll see it's not just a face. It has an eagle up top, and the eagle has his wings wrapped around the Indian, protecting him."

"And it has *nothing* to do with a totem pole!"

Toth emphasizes that last bit a lot. In conversation, his words float on a friendly Midwestern lilt. But I sensed a bit of an edge when it comes to the totem pole issue. Yes, Toth's statues are tall. Yes, they're carved from trees. Yes, they represent major figures from individual tribes.

And no, they are definitely not totem poles.

"If you want to see totem poles, you should probably go up to the Pacific Northwest and Alaska, which are the only places Native Americans make them," he says.

"But people still come to my studio and say, 'Hey, you're the guy who takes telephone poles and makes totem poles out of 'em!'

"I tell 'em 'Thank you.' But they're ignoramuses."

If Toth, now 71, seems a little defensive, it's understandable. As he speaks from his studio south of Daytona Beach, Florida, he has just opened a *National Geographic* magazine article that derisively lumps him in with opportunistic artists who appropriate Native American symbols and motifs to make a quick buck.

Toth actually agrees with the article's disdain for such rip-offs, which he says are created largely by "white assholes."

"I make the statues to honor American Indians," he says. "I make each one in a composite likeness of the local indigenous people, and I donate them to every state."

Toth never even starts a project without consulting closely with local tribes. And if you're wondering how Native Americans feel about his work, just consider his middle name, which was bestowed on him by the Eastern band of the Cherokee nation.

"Does every Indian like my work? Of course not!" he says. "It's art! I can't speak for individuals, but in general the reaction is very positive."

Born in Hungary but raised in Akron, Ohio, Toth was inspired to begin sculpting Indians in 1972, when on a West Coast jaunt he saw a sandstone cliff at the beach in La Jolla, California. Without asking permission, Toth started chipping away at the outcropping, explaining to a cop he was "releasing a face of a haunted Indian."

The officer must have been an art lover: He let Toth finish the face, which gazes out over the Pacific to this day.

Returning to Ohio, Toth was determined to sculpt another rock-faced Indian, but there was one problem: Ohio doesn't have much in the way of cliffs.

"I did find a cliff in a rock quarry," he says, "but only some squirrels and raccoons would ever have seen my statue."

"Then one day I was driving with my girlfriend through a park in Akron, and I saw this dead elm tree. It was perfect! I went to the parks people and asked them, 'How about if I donate a statue to you guys?' They said 'Wonderful!'"

The art critics arrived early.

"This jerk came up and started cursing at me," Toth recalls. "He was saying 'What are you doing? You're killing a tree!' I said, 'Hey man, this tree was dead when I got here.' Then he said, 'Well, I love to see dead trees rotting!' So I run into all kinds of critics."

Still, Toth had found his medium.

"I started to think, 'This is even better than stone! I'm intertwining the spirit of the Indians with the spirit of the tree!'"

But wood does rot. In fact, that first carved tree in Akron is long gone.

And it's happened in Bethany — twice. Toth's first iteration of Chief Little Owl, dedicated in 1976, was destroyed in a 1992 windstorm, weakened by termites. You can still see remains of it at the Nanticoke Indian Museum in Long Neck. Pennsylvania chainsaw artist Dennis Beach created a replacement, but that one barely lasted eight years before it was ruined by rot. That brought Toth back to town. His re-do, which stands to this day, is made from an extra hard log imported from totem pole country in the Pacific Northwest.

Third Time's The Charm

Toth estimates the wood should last 50-100 years, but this time around the Nanticoke didn't take any chances. At the 2002 dedication ceremony, the work was blessed by Charlie Clark, a descendant of Chief Little Owl.

So far, so good: Fifteen years later Chief Little Owl doesn't seem the worse for wear. If you look closely, you'll see a little canvas cap on the eagle's head, a shield against deposits from seagulls.

Still, Toth says, he'd like to come back and give the chief a little touch-up.

"Even western red cedar won't endure without the proper preservative," he says. "If they'd invite me back I'd like to put a little stain on. Not paint – just a little light color."

When he's not on the road sculpturing Whispering Giants — or scouting sites for new works on the Amazon, in Israel, and on the Danube — you'll find Toth, sporting a backwards baseball cap and a healthy handlebar mustache, painting canvases or chipping away at wood at his Florida studio. The grounds are punctuated by hundreds of sculptures of all sizes, which leads some passers-by to think they can come in and order up a work just the right size for an empty corner of their living rooms.

"It doesn't work like that," he says. "I get a piece of wood, and I just remove everything that doesn't belong there."

Indian River Inlet Taunted Humans for Centuries Until This Abridged Version

MIND THE GAP

Those of us who are relatively new to coastal Delaware can be forgiven for cruising across the drop-dead gorgeous Indian River Bridge and saying to ourselves, "How nice of God to give us this lovely, well-defined and clearly permanent inlet for our fishing and driving pleasure!"

But the truth is, left to its natural state the Indian River Inlet is anything but permanent. In fact, before the Army Corps of Engineers dredged the channel and defined it with two walls of giant rocks in 1939, the inlet roamed up and down the coastline like an old guy with a metal detector.

The long sliver of sand that links Dewey with Bethany isn't a barrier island *per se*, but it acts just like one. The sea built it, the sea can wash it away — and frequently it does.

For millennia, inlets came and went here, carved at the whims of major storms.

The wanderings of this opening to the ocean probably explain why archaeologists have never found evidence of a permanent pre-Columbian settlement in the area. Why set up shop when next week there could be a river running through your living room?

In the 1800s alone, the inlet moved from approximately where it is now to another spot about one mile north, then to another location about a quarter-mile north of that. By the 1930s it had migrated back down to its present location, where the Corps of Engineers decided to etch it in stone, literally.

I am studying a map of those meanderings, drawn in 1882. It hangs in the Indian River Life-Saving Station Museum, and as I bend closer to get a good look at the details, I wonder aloud what's to prevent Mother Nature from opening a new inlet.

"Nothing, really," says Laura Scharle, the museum's interpretive programs manager. "All it takes is a big storm. We just haven't had one in a while.

"Plus, there's no reason why there has to be just one inlet. Sometimes there have been more than one; sometimes there has been no inlet at all."

Compared to other stations up and down the coast, she says, "this one was busier than most of the others because of the inlet. It just kept moving and the channels kept shifting. Plus, the inlet was quite shallow, so there were a lot of shipwrecks."

The inlet has wrecked several bridges, too. In the early days of the automobile, if you wanted to drive from Rehoboth Beach to Bethany Beach, you had to take the inland route through Millsboro. A wooden bridge was thrown across the shallow, unpredictable inlet in 1934, but it barely lasted four years. Then a succession of swing bridges went up over the next couple of decades, but they were brought down by ice floes.

A steel girder bridge, built in 1965, endured for nearly 50 years before the beautiful new cable-stayed model opened in 2012.

There's no more picturesque walk in coastal Delaware than a stroll across the Indian River Inlet Bridge (officially the

Charles W. Cullen Bridge — all but the first bridge iteration have been named after the longtime Delaware Supreme Court justice). From the center of the span, where the inlet waters rush directly below, the sweeping vista includes a spectacular view of the northern beach, awash in lacy white breakers, all the way to the horizon. The beach to the south is hidden by dunes and the retractable umbrella of The Big Chill restaurant — but seen from the air, that beach often extends nearly twice as far into the sea as the northern one.

For that, blame the inlet: Prevailing currents carry sand from the south, and those rock jetties block the flow, starving the north beach of new sand.

If nothing were done, the upper beach would erode all the way to Route 1. But never underestimate the resourcefulness of a determined engineer: For much of the year, a machine sucks up sand from the southern beach, pumps it across the bridge through a huge pipe, and re-deposits it on the deprived north side.

Clearly, people have been pondering the Indian River Inlet for centuries — but it's safe to say no one has given the place more thought than Mohammad Keshtpoor. As a graduate student at the University of Delaware's coastal engineering school, Keshtpoor spent five years studying the dynamics of the inlet for his Ph.D. dissertation.

These days Keshtpoor works as a storm surge expert for a San Francisco risk management company — but when I track him down by phone, he is clearly thrilled to revisit the channel that he obsessed over for half a decade.

"It's a fantastic place!" he enthuses. "Any time you get so much water moving in such a confined space, amazing things happen."

From that perch at the middle of the Indian River Bridge, you're seeing just a small fraction of the pure power being unleashed by the tidal forces that push water inland into Rehoboth Bay, then out to sea. Just below the surface, Keshtpoor excitedly tells me, the turbulent waters of the Indian River Inlet explode with ferocious violence.

"It has been calculated that the amount of water that leaves Rehoboth Bay at ebb tide is 525 million cubic feet," he says.

That sounds like a lot of water. And it is.

"Imagine a soccer field," he says, barely containing his delight. "Now, imagine that soccer field covered in water to a height of 7,000 feet."

That's right: The water coursing out to sea through the inlet each day would create a column the width and length of a soccer field and the height of six Empire State Buildings.

All that fast-moving water is going to do a lot of damage — and it's happening deep within the channel.

Attached to Keshtpoor's doctoral thesis are some colorful bathymetric charts of the inlet — the underwater equivalent of topographic maps. The darker the color on those charts, the deeper the water: Just under the bridge the chart's light color indicates a depth of 15 feet or so. But at either end of the channel, in the bay and in the Atlantic, the color darkens to the deep purple of a grievous bruise.

Each bruise marks the spot where the rushing waters have scoured two holes, measuring at least 100 feet deep — deeper than any spot in Delaware Bay. Were it not for the still-submerged pilings of the previous bridge interrupting the flow of water, the inlet would be 100 feet deep from end to end.

And those holes are not cut into soft sand.

"Below about 30 feet, under the sand, you find clay — something called consolidated cohesive sediment," says Keshtpoor. "It's almost as hard as concrete. And the deeper you go, the harder it gets.

"So the water from the inlet has carved two holes, each 100 feet deep. Into concrete."

The gush of tides through Indian River Inlet also tells another story — one that extends far beyond the waters of coastal Delaware.

"Between 1976 and 1994," Keshtpoor says, "the Army Corps of Engineers measured an increase of water velocity through the channel of about 2 percent. Higher velocity means a higher amount of water going through.

"I suspect if you were to measure that velocity last year, and then again this year, you'd get an increase of even more. Can you guess why that might be?"

I haven't been expecting a quiz, but I have an idea.

"Rising sea levels?" I guess.

"Exactly!" he says. "A very smart answer!"

As one who usually asks the questions, I feel a surprising wave of satisfaction.

"This is not opinion," he continues. "These are devices measuring it. Sea levels are rising."

It seems like a somber note on which to end our chat, but Keshtpoor keeps his insistently enthusiastic attitude. Water is his life, and the Indian River Inlet is all about water.

Coming over the crest of the bridge, I head north. To my right, beyond the tall sand dunes that help keep waves from carving out rogue inlets along this stretch of beach, the relentless surf keeps up its endless barrage. To my left lurks a sheen of brackish water — barely visible around the roots of marsh plants. There it waits to launch regular rear guard assaults on the Route 1 roadbed — which in recent years has been raised a few pitiful inches in vertical retreat from the rising bay.

For now, we humans are keeping our tenuous grip on this narrow spit of sand. As always, we think we're in charge. And as always, we sooner or later learn we are not.

A Cornfield Gets an Earfull

LET US SPRAY

The sound awoke me, and even before my brain kicked into gear, I recognized it: The dive-bomb roar... the seconds of near silence ... the renewed urgency of an airplane swinging into another approach.

It was unmistakable. There was a crop duster in the neighborhood. And he was very close.

Yanking jeans over my pajama shorts, I grabbed the car keys and shouted an incomprehensible explanation to my wife (Carolyn's used to this by now). Driving out to the main road, I stopped, rolled open all the car's windows and the sunroof, and tried to discern precisely where the sound was coming from.

Then I saw him. Above a ridge of trees, the yellow glint of a biplane's wings caught the early morning sun. It took some maneuvering through unfamiliar roads, but finally there he was in full view, swooping like a lemon-colored condor over a Robinsonville Road cornfield.

I spotted the pilot, his yellow helmet clearly visible through a window, and marveled at his dramatic approach — how he seemed to leap from behind the tree line before plummeting to just a few feet above the corn, nearly close enough to reach out and run his hand along the waving stalks. My eyes tried to track him as he skimmed the surface at 150 miles per hour, and I held my breath as he barreled right towards the power lines along Webbs Landing Road. Surely he'd cleared wires like that a thousand times, I told myself, and surely he'd do it again.

He did. With inches to spare, it seemed. Then, in a wide, graceful turn, the biplane disappeared to the north.

I was sorry to see him go. Even in the seven short years I've lived here, I've noticed that visits from the crop dusters are becoming less frequent. The day seems close when, after the last cornfields have been smothered by concrete and clubhouses, crop dusters will no longer come to us. We'll have to go to them.

And that's just what I'm doing. It is now a few days later, and I have followed that little yellow plane to its home base: Chorman Airport, about 30 miles northwest of Rehoboth in Greenwood. It is 5 a.m. on the Fourth of July, but the place is buzzing with activity as a small army of workers tinkers with engines, mixes chemicals, and rolls open hangar doors to reveal a virtual air force of agricultural aircraft. The windsock atop the main hangar droops limply, and in the still, inky light of pre-dawn, the air is a mix of fertilizer and aviation fuel.

"I hear it's a holiday today," says Jeff Chorman with a wry smile when I meet up with him in the break room. Chorman runs the day-to-day business of Allen Chorman & Son Inc., established three decades ago by his dad.

The senior Chorman, now 73, is something of an aviation legend in these parts. Tributes to him line the walls of this room: certificates from the State of Delaware and Sussex County honoring his contributions to agriculture. Allen began piloting crop dusters for longtime Sussex County aviator Joe

Hudson in the 1960s, flying out of Rehoboth Airport — which is these days commemorated by the names of the streets that once served it: Airport Road and Cessna Drive.

Allen bought the business from Hudson in 1987. Jeff, who's 40 now, started flying crop dusters for his dad when he was 18, in high school.

Together, the Chormans and their staff have buzzed virtually every farm field on the Delmarva Peninsula. Since the 1990s they've owned this airstrip — plus some 20 aircraft, including a helicopter.

As I describe how I stalked his employee in the yellow biplane that recent morning, Jeff smiles and shakes his head. Overzealous observers have no idea, he says, how much trouble they cause his pilots.

"It happens all the time — they get in the way!" he says with a laugh, but he clearly means it. "Sometimes people hang out on the downwind side of the field, and everything's blowing towards them.

"Eventually you have to fly away to make them think you're done. Then you come back when they're gone."

Remembering how the yellow biplane had abruptly left the scene as I jockeyed below him taking pictures that morning along Robinsonville Road, I summon up an apology. But Chorman waves me off. He enjoys his work too much to let distractions like me ruin it for him.

"I just love the flying," he says. Then he offers to take me up and show me why.

The sun is just revealing itself on the eastern horizon as we walk past an array of yellow single-seater airplanes, each mounted with a spray unit under its wings. From a large hangar, a worker on a cart has just towed out a twin-engine Beechcraft. It's the company's biggest plane — and also its oldest, by a long shot, a decommissioned U.S. Coast Guard duster that's been airborne since 1943.

I climb up the plane's fold-out stairway and inch past two large plastic containers filled with insecticide: We're heading to kill mosquitoes at the Trail's End campground near Wallops

Island, Va., about 80 miles south. The dashboard is defiantly analog, with an array of dials and switches Gregory Peck might have fiddled with in "Twelve O'Clock High."

"The whole reason I ever wanted to be an ag pilot was to fly these twin Beeches," Chorman says. "I used to ride in 'em with my dad when I was 10-12 years old. I'd look at him sitting there, and I'd think he was God."

Faster than I expected, we're airborne, swinging around to the south. Chorman has issued me a pair of earplugs, but even with them and the yellow safety helmet, the roar of the right engine — just a few feet outside my open window — is deafening.

As the farms and small towns of the mid-peninsula slide past beneath us, I squint to the east, trying to catch a glimpse of the Delaware beaches. A ribbon of silver shines on the Atlantic, and for a moment I mourn the fact that I didn't live in coastal Sussex County when it was still green and rural.

"There's very little farmland left over there," Chorman tells me later — the engine is too loud for any kind of conversation while airborne. "Along Route 1 from Five Points South — that was the best farmland in the state."

Still, for anyone concerned that agriculture may be evicted from the region anytime soon, the view from 500 feet is reassuring: As far as I can see the land is a patchwork quilt of farms away from the coast, interrupted by the occasional long, low chicken shed.

Somewhere east of Seaford, Chorman removes his hands from the pilot's yoke and gestures toward the one that's sitting in front of me. It had never occurred to me he might let me take the wheel. Uncertainly, I assume control, and in that moment I recall a long-forgotten childhood dream, one that was born one Saturday morning watching "Sky King" on television. I'm flying.

Gently, I ease the yoke to the right, and I feel us tipping, ever so slightly. I have the presence of mind to glance over at the attitude indicator, in front of Chorman. Sure enough, the little white plane on the indicator is following my lead, first to the right, then to the left. Too soon, Chorman resumes control of the plane, but it's just as well. I have no idea where we're going.

Soon the seaward side of the peninsula bends in to meet us, and Chorman brings us in to barely 100 feet up. We cross the marshy shoreline of Chincoteague Bay, double back, and head for the expansive stand of trees that shades the mobile homes and campsites at Trail's End. To the folks down there, the Doppler effect raises the pitch of the engine's sound as we approach, then lowers it as we pass, just like war planes in the movies. To us, the engine's drone remains constant.

We're making six passes over Trail's End — a milk run for Chorman, who's accustomed to spraying land parcels far larger than this one. Each time we bank to the left over the bay, I look to the pilot's seat and see nothing but Chorman's profile and, below him, sun-dappled water.

We are heading back north, but Chorman wants to show me one more thing before we land. On his smartphone — for this is how we must communicate despite sitting side by side — he types out: "I'm going to take us over a field as if we're crop dusting."

The Beechcraft skims the treetops of a wooded area. Beyond I can see a large field carpeted with low-lying string beans. As soon as we pass the trees, about 100 feet up, the Beech plunges into a deep dive, and in what seems like less than a second we're barreling across the field at 150 miles per hour.

We are eight feet above the ground. A six-foot farmer raising his hand in our path would risk losing it. The furrows of beans extend straight ahead, close enough for me to make out individual leaves 50 feet or so ahead but becoming nothing but a blur as the plane passes directly over them.

We are approaching another stand of trees, one that moments ago seemed very far away. The Beech pulls up like a rearing horse. The view outside the windshield is a whirl of beans, tree trunks, leaves and sky. Simultaneous with our ascent, Chorman is already banking, preparing for the next pass. I am completely disoriented, literally unaware of up, down, or sideways.

I am as thrilled as I've ever been in my life.

Too soon, we're on the ground again. My pilot is back in the break room chatting with a colleague about today's jobs: more mosquitoes near Dover, nearly 200 acres of string beans on three different farms and a cornfield in Liepsic. And that's just before lunch. Later he'll be fertilizing corn in Sudlersville, Md., and potatoes in Hurlock, also in the neighboring state. He hopes to be back home in Broadkill to watch the Fourth of July fireworks with his wife and two daughters.

"You need a lot of equipment and dedication to succeed in this business," he adds. "But mostly, you need a very understanding wife."

And then he is out the door. Those string beans won't spray themselves.

A Man And His Pond

THE POND GUY

If you live in a southern Delaware housing community, you may well have had the experience of gazing out your back window and seeing one or two guys pushing into your pond in a flat-bottomed rowboat, like Pogo and Albert Alligator heading off for an expedition in the Okefenokee Swamp.

Wait a minute," you tell yourself. "*I* want to go boating in my pond! When did the homeowners association approve *that*?"

Don't even think about it. Almost certainly, those are not pleasure boaters at all but drainage pond specialists who are looking after the health and well-being of your ponds and, consequently, your well being — not to mention your property values.

Todd Fritchman grew up snorkeling along Duck Creek near Smyrna and spent much of his childhood at his family's second home in Rehoboth Beach. With two degrees in biology, including a master's in aquatics, he brings unusual expertise to his work as president of Envirotech, a firm that maintains hundreds of drainage ponds in developments throughout coastal Delaware.

I met up with Fritchman at the edge of Silver Lake in Rehoboth Beach, where he gave me a primer in the surprisingly unknown watery realms that lie just beyond everyone's back door.

Like lots of successful professionals, Fritchman has an uncommon enthusiasm for something the rest of us take for granted.

"There's so much going on in these ponds that people don't know," he says with a level of excitement most children reserve for discussions about Santa Claus.

"In fact, there's a representative of every kind of animal in the animal kingdom in your pond — except for humans, of course."

As one who grew up in New Jersey, I'm about to debate that last point, but I decide against it.

"Besides the animals you can readily see, like birds and aquatic mammals like muskrats, you have moneras (single-cell bacteria) and protists (single-cell animal/plant hybrids) and aquatic fungus," he continues. "You have freshwater clams. Because it's fresh water, instead of jellyfish you have little aquatic polyps called hydras. You need a microscope to see them, but they're there."

Fritchman casts his gaze across Silver Lake — one of just two natural lakes in the whole state of Delaware. The other one happens to be just across town; Lake Gerar. Every other lake-like body of water in the state is, technically, a pond: a wide spot in a stream created by building a dam.

"Ordinarily, this lake is one of the best large mouth bass fisheries in the world, and I mean the entire planet," he says. "But it has gone through two major fish kills.

"It had a lot to do with uncontrolled sediment erosion — people building houses blocks away from here, leaving piles of dirt out in the street, and the rain washing the silt and sediment all down into Silver Lake. You get suspended clay particles in the water, fungus grows on it, and the oxygen levels in the water crash. We had 800,000 dead whitefish in this lake."

When I first moved to Delaware, the big debate in my development was over the grass growing around the ponds. The county and state say you're supposed to let natural plants sprout up along the shoreline, but lots of my neighbors couldn't understand why it couldn't be manicured right up to the water, like a golf course. Fritchman hears this all the time.

"Golf courses are designed specifically to allow grass up to the edge," he tells me. "Among other things, that involves irrigating the grass all the way out, so it takes root and prevents erosion.

"And you know, the fact is not everyone wants that golf course look. A lot of people like having a native plant barrier. Some people even want us to make the plant barrier wider than it already is!"

I don't know any of *those* people, but it's nice to know they're out there.

A Tricky Lie (Photo by Carolyn Newcott)

PUTT 'ER THERE:
OUR TOUGHEST MINI GOLF HOLES

Maybe they can't match the 8th hole at Pebble Beach for difficulty, but good mini golf courses have their own ways of frustrating even seasoned players. I visited each of Coastal Delaware's courses and invited the staffs to point me to their most challenging holes.

Fire Mountain Mini Golf
Route 1, Midway
   11th Hole: "Morne Aux Diables" (Devil's Peak)
   Par 4: Player: Bogey
A groundskeeper at Fire Mountain seems to take offense when I ask him to point me to the course's most difficult hole.

"It's designed for fun!" he says sternly. "It's for children!" Add a Scottish accent and I could mistake him for Groundskeeper Willie on *The Simpsons*.

Which doesn't make me feel any better about being totally flummoxed by the course's 11th hole, named for a volcano on the island of Dominica. On one hand it's a classic two-tiered hole, with a pair of drains on the upper level, each of which lands the ball at a different spot on the green. On the other hand, both holes are hidden from the putter by a pair of wooden pier pilings.

It takes two strokes for me to get the ball into the hole on the right, which at first glance seems like the better choice. Sure enough, the pipeline sends the ball rolling in the direction of the hole, but it misses by a few inches, bounces off the low barrier wall, and rebounds into a wedge of stones, where it gets hopelessly lodged. It costs me a stroke to pull it out, guaranteeing a bogey.

A second try on the upper level gets the ball in the left hole, which after a long trip through a subterranean pipe is spit out some 10 feet closer to the hole than the first one. From there it was an easy birdie.

Free Game Hole: Fire Mountain's bonus game hole, with a trench that sucks in most putts, is also its 18th. **Difficulty:** It's the hardest one around. To win, a putter must drive the ball all the way up a chicken coop-type ramp with no barriers on either side. "About two or three people a day get it," says staffer Denise McCoy.

Shell We Golf?
Route 1, Rehoboth Beach
17th Hole: "The Humps"
Par 4: Player: Six Strokes (unofficial maximum)
Just one hole shy of the 18th green at the lushly landscaped Shell We Golf, the simple oval green that surrounds the 17th cup looks positively mulligan-like.

Not so fast, Arnold Palmer. Check out the humps. They surround the hole in a random manner, ready to send even the most perfectly hit ball squiggling off in an unexpected direction.

"This is the one people could spend all night on," says manager John Derrick. "They get faked out by how easy it looks."

Unless they're lucky enough to get a totally unearned hole in one, players trying to negotiate the 17th hole must first place their putt so the ball ends up with a clear line to the hole between two humps. Trying to sink a putt over a hump is a duffer's delusion; there's no telling where the ball will roll to a stop. It's a maddening bit of calculus that more often than not leaves players swatting the ball back and forth until waiting golfers scream for them to just pick it up.

Free Game Hole: A trench on the 19th hole will swallow ball unless you sink it in the cup. In that case a bell rings and you get a free game. **Difficulty:** Some 20-30 golfers a day get a freebie.

Ryan's Mini Golf
Rehoboth Beach Boardwalk
16th Hole: "The Red Light"
Par 2   Player: Double Bogey

Like the infamously windy Ginger Beer hole at St. Andrews' Old Course, the Red Light at Ryan's Mini Golf inspires headaches for golfers who watch helplessly as a stiff sea breeze can blow even the most perfectly executed putt sideways.

"All it takes is a sudden squall and everything up here is blowing all over the place," says Denise Kirn, whose family has owned the rooftop course for five years.

In a non-scientific poll of players one recent evening, Kirn deduced that the most difficult hole was number 15, the Orange Mermaid, which requires a perfectly placed angle shot on an incline to get good placement near the hole.

But the Red Light hole offers unique challenges of its own, not the least of which is its location closest to the windy sea. Also, the hole offers a variation on the classic windmill challenge: a slowly turning railway-like semaphore periodically fully blocks the single passage to the hole, requiring both aim and timing on the part of the golfer.

Free Game Hole: The 19th hole requires players to launch their putt into a bulls-eye. **Difficulty:** "Pretty easy, I guess — we give away about 20 free games a day," says Kirn. "Little kids are best at it — they're not trying as hard."

Captain Jack's Pirate Golf
Pennsylvania Avenue, Bethany Beach
3rd Hole: "The Monkey's Loose"
No Official Par (Player: Six Strokes, Official Maximum)

Each hole at this compact course has an official sponsor. In this case I'm sure the Maloney Family are very nice people, but I'm hoping they're not as sneaky as the hole that bears their name.

It looks simple enough: A conventional horseshoe with a steep slope up toward the bend, followed by another slope to the left, down to the green. The player slaps the ball up the hill, hoping to land it there for a clear putt down the other side. Of course, if the ball is not hit hard enough it will come rolling back. But hit the ball too hard and it will plop into a stream of running water and float away

Desperate to avoid a watery end, I persist in tapping the ball up the hill, and four times it returns to me. On my fifth stroke I hit it too hard and, to my dismay, it rolls right into the water.

Then it floats downstream a few feet and runs into a small barrier that feeds the ball directly onto the green. The wet ball rolls to within a few inches of the cup.

As Captain Jack might say, "Aaargh!"

Free Game Hole: Launch your ball beyond the ball-swallowing trench on the 18th hole and you get a free game. "There are two holes," a father explains to his son. "A hole for winners, and a hole for losers." **Difficulty:** Turns out there are lots of winners: Captain Jack hands out 10-15 free games a day.

Viking Golf & Go Carts
Virginia Avenue, Fenwick Island
8th Hole: "The Troll Tree"
Par 2 Player: Double Bogey

Perhaps it's the distraction of the bearded troll peering out from Viking Golf's landmark gnarly tree, presiding over the course's deceptively easy looking 8th hole. I simply cannot seem to find the cup.

In fact, at first I can't even see the cup — it's hidden from the tee by a large rock. All I see is a sweeping, inclined curve that extends under the curly "roots" of that fiberglass tree. I get tangled up in the roots momentarily, then my ball skids down to a barely-visible valley at the far end of the green.

Somehow I sink my putt from there, saving myself the humiliation of having to pick up on my fifth stroke. I'm sure I would have been trolled by the troll.

Free Game Hole: "The Cracken" is an intimidating downhill hole that, when perfectly played, launches your ball into the toothy maw of a legendary monster. Otherwise, a long trench claims your ball. **Difficulty:** Those stoic Vikings don't give up their free games easily. On most days just five players win, says my guide Meriah Bruch.

Nick's "Golf Down Under" Mini Golf
Delaware 54, Fenwick Island
9th Hole: "Straightaway"
No Official Par (Player, 4 strokes)

I've never seen a mini golf hole as long and straight as the 9th at Nick's. I'm tempted to literally tee off, but that could easily send my ball into the next state — literally, since the course sits smack on the Delaware-Maryland state line. Of course, that would require clearing the gigantic replica of Australia's Uluru (Ayers Rock), one of many touches that enhance Nick's Down Under theme.

The fairway is straight, but it has several tiers — three drops and then one rise — that complicate any attempt to make a clean putt. I get stuck in the midsection, and am lucky to emerge with what I consider a bogey.

The course attendant, Seth Bishop, suggests I try the hole fondly called "Dolly Parton" — featuring two prominent mounds on either side of the fairway. But I find that if I simply putt down the middle, the cleavage shunts me right to the cup. Which is no bigger than any normal cup, I might add.

Free Game Hole: The 18th hole at Nick's Down Under is no gimme: You putt the ball from an elevation and watch it make a long, looping figure 8 journey toward the green. Everyone plays for the same hole, but if you sink it in one stroke you win a free game. No bells or lights signify a winner: "We can just tell by how excited everyone gets," Bishop says. **Difficulty:** Four or five players have a g'day each day.

A Prize-Winning Delaware Ducker

SAILS OF THE CENTURIES

The 20-foot-long, cobalt blue lake canoe occupies much of the length of David Greenhaugh's driveway. Even to a guy who doesn't know a dinghy from a deck boat, the workmanship is striking, the artisan's attention to detail unmistakable.

Just above the bow, the canoe's triangular deck plate — made of hard cherry wood — is stained like a fine piece of living room furniture. Inside the canoe, the gloss of white paint is smooth enough to see my reflection.

Between the white inside and blue exterior, embedded in the long, sweeping starboard gunwale at the top of the hull, a thin red strip of stained wood runs its entire length. This is the only evidence that the shell of this canoe is constructed entirely of redwood.

"I cut the strips myself in my workshop," Greenhaugh says, running his hand along the smooth ridge.

I imagine Greenhaugh setting to work on a pile of choice lumber. In my mind's eye he hews long lengths of virgin redwood, freshly timbered from the American Northwest.

Then he says, "It used to be a pickle barrel."

Assuming this is some sort of nautical joke, I laugh.

"No, really," he smiles. "I found this huge old pickle barrel in Atlanta, about 14 feet in diameter and probably 10 feet deep. It took many truckloads to get the wood up here.

"I cut it down into strips. I narrowed it into a quarter-inch by five-sixteenths, I guess. And I started from there."

With painstaking precision and unfathomable patience, Greenhaugh glued each flexible strip onto a frame. When the last piece was set in place, he had a canoe.

He bends a bit, tilting his head so his eye can trace the gentle arc of the gunwale.

"It's a good boat," he says. And Greenhaugh should know. He's owned "eight or 12" boats and built three of them.

If you want to know how long they've been building good boats in this neighborhood, look no farther than the Lewes History Museum. There, behind a glass panel, you'll find the remains of a 600-year-old dugout canoe, discovered in a local marsh. It's typical of the canoes built by the Nanticoke people, and as the name suggests, it was crafted by literally digging out the trunk of a felled tree.

The broad tree trunk canoes of Delaware's first native peoples were the precursors to later fishing and hunting boats built by subsequent generations of coastal Delawareans. Also in the Lewes History Museum is a broad-bottomed 1910 Delaware Ducker, shallow enough to negotiate the local swamplands; stable enough for a hunter to stand on its deck and fire a shotgun at flying fowl.

Variations of the Delaware Ducker plied the swampy coastal waters up and down the Eastern seaboard. Most were built by their owners after eyeballing a neighbor's boat, so in a nautical version of the whispering game Telephone the details of each craft could be subtly different. That's how an expert can tell the difference between a New Jersey Ducker and a Delaware one.

In the mid 1600s, before Lewes got its name, a Dutch shipwright named Cornelis Verhoef was hammering away off the waters of Canary Creek. By 1683 — after William Penn claimed the three counties on the Delaware River as part of Pennsylvania — the Brits got in on the act. Shipwrights William Beverly and John Brown began launching new boats into Lewes' natural harbor, the creek below what is now Shipcarpenter Street.

Shipbuilding in Lewes really took off in the 18th Century, with three or four major shipyard operations — including one operated by Cato Lewis, a former African slave who had bought his freedom, and his son Peter — turning out moderate-sized ships, including at least one major schooner capable of carrying up to 72 tons of cargo. Where today children swing in the playground and couples walk arm-in-arm on the graveled paths of Canalfront Park, for centuries burly guys toiled, tools in hand, over the growing frames of ships under construction.

It took a lot of lumber to build those ships, and there were plenty of trees growing right nearby. But de-forestation led to land erosion, accelerating silting of the creek. The water became too shallow for launching larger craft, so by the late 1800s the center of Sussex County ship building had shifted up the Broadkill River to Milton. Lewes never reclaimed the shipbuilding fame it once had.

But that was just a stopgap strategy: the die had been cast for the local ship industry. Coastal Delaware's rivers were too silted, the channels too shallow, the demand for ever-larger vessels too insistent. The professional shipbuilders moved on, leaving empty shorelines and, in all likelihood, layers of bottles, coins, and tools sinking in the sediment below their old worksites.

The shipyards may have vanished from coastal Delaware, but the ship builders never did. Hunters still crafted their duck boats. Crabbers still built their skiffs. And still others, dipping into that primeval urge to become one with the sea, simply built boats because, well, that's how you get out into the water.

David Greenhaugh's Really Big Canoe

That's what drives David Greenhaugh, the man with the 20-foot canoe in his driveway. We shake hands — my spindly writer's fingers disappearing into the mitts of a guy who makes his living as a mechanic. After I've admired his workmanship, he invites me inside for a cup of coffee.

Appropriate to the location of his house just off Pilottown Road, Greenhaugh is a former local river pilot. A lifelong resident, for years he helped guide ships as they ventured beyond Cape Henlopen and up the Delaware.

As the morning sun reflects off the Lewes Canal outside his front room window, Greenhaugh tells me he built his first boat about 15 years ago. Like the canoe outside, it was strip-built: made of small pieces of wood glued together and stapled on a frame.

"Next, I built a dinghy for that boat," he says, indicating a painting on the wall behind me. I turn to see the image of a handsome wood fishing boat moored to a rocky shoreline. And sure enough, standing on its side at the aft end is a small dinghy. The large boat has long since been sold and now resides in New England.

"The dinghy is in the basement," he says, and he takes me downstairs to visit it.

Mounted hull-up on two wooden benches in Greenhaugh's spotless basement is the vessel, a rounded rowboat small enough to sit on the deck of a ship.

"The larger boat was named *Rain Dog*, and the dinghy is named *Pup*," he says, tilting it to one side. "This one's built of plywood. I put these steps here so my dog could get in and out. I can just about get it through that door over there."

Greenhaugh's masterpiece, though, is that long, wide-bottomed beauty in the driveway. Her name is *Ora*, and she's similar in size to ones in which the Iroquois once plied the waters of Lake Champlain.

"I built it because I had paddled a 14-foot canoe down the Broadkill one February, and my dog kept jumping from one side to the other to see birds. I thought I was gonna tip! So I decided to build a canoe that wouldn't flip over."

He spent about 500 hours crafting *Ora* over a six-month period.

"When you're building a strip boat like that, you work on it piece by piece," he says. "You can work on it for a half-hour and then take days off — or you can work on it for days and take a half-hour off."

For Greenhaugh, building a boat is a means to an end: getting it into the water and sailing off in it.

"The best thing about building a boat is finishing it," he says.

There's no doubt Neil Stevenson loves sailing on the boats he builds, but one look at his meticulously drafted plans — with finely drawn lines and hundreds of intricate notations accurate to a quarter of an inch — and you know the process of creation is every bit as precious to him.

We are standing at Stevenson's drafting table in a well-lit room at the rear of his house in Rehoboth Beach. It's the house of a boat builder; a wide-open space with beautifully finished, bare wooden beams that resemble below decks on a 19th Century frigate. There's not a nail to be seen: Stevenson built the entire house using pegs.

"I've built about 12 boats," he says. "I still have some of them, including the best one I ever built: a 22-foot tri hull. That's on a trailer. I've got a 25-foot catamaran at anchor. I have a motorboat in the yard.

"I also built a 12 ½-foot Herreshoff tender that I have out back. It's a real classic design, the kind the Herreshoff company would build for you if you got one of their yachts. When I sailed to Florida on my 24-foot tri hull I had that tender on the deck, and these guys in million-dollar sailboats would all yell, 'Nice boat!' They weren't talking about my tri hull; they were talking about my tender."

Stevenson, a lifelong surfer who spent years working on pilot boats, has been sailing for 42 years — most often his own boats, but frequently transporting other people's crafts. He's a living encyclopedia of boat engineering, freely quoting Howard I. Chapelle, author of the recognized bible of boat building. He holds forth on the benefits of epoxy resin over polyester glue for affixing slats. But after all the prevailing and classic design theories have been consulted, for Stevenson it all comes down to one thing: Does it *look* right?

"I've read Chapelle cover to cover, all about lofting and measurements and diagonals," he says. "I say, 'Nah, that's too much trouble.' I just take a flexible wooden baton and bend it until it looks right, and then build from there."

He's a big fan of trial and error, too.

"For my first boat, I just started bolting together pieces of junk boats. Built it from scratch. It was a really cool boat, but it was a failure — it didn't have enough floatation or wave clearance."

When he'd scraped together enough spare money from his work in construction and as a handyman, in 2002 Stevenson got busy building his second boat.

"I took into account all the failures of my first boat, and the second boat was a success," he says. "That's the one I think is my best ever."

His eyes fixed on his latest design — a project that's been gestating for a couple of years now — Stevenson considers whether his heart is most set on sailing boats or building them.

"Honestly," he finally says, "I guess I'm more interested in figuring it out."

Bob Reed rolls up the garage door to his workshop, located below a Rehoboth Beach rental house he owns. Like the other boat builders I've met, Reed's projects unfold at a site remote from his home. As the door slides up, the smell of untreated wood floats through my nostrils.

I immediately see three boats — two smaller wooden ones and, toward the back, a fiberglass sailing craft.

"I built this little hunting boat and this tender," he says. The latter is a striking small boat, painted white inside and out. Seen from the rear, the profile of each individual glued plywood strip is clearly visible. Each one flares out a bit, making the two sides resemble the outline of an angel's wings.

"I scarfed the planks together," he says. "You can scarf two pieces of wood by tapering them, so if you have two half-inch thick pieces of wood you taper them from full thickness to nothing. Then you put the two pieces together and use epoxy to glue them."

Reed built the boat 10 years ago. I mention that it still looks seaworthy. "Eh, I don't really have a lot of confidence in it," he says. "Epoxy has a tendency to unzip — molecule by molecule it just comes apart."

So, we won't be going out in that one. He would, however, trust the hunting boat, a little number he built nearly 20 years ago.

"It's cedar on frame, and rather than caulking the joints I put epoxy and cloth on it all the way around" he says. "You'd carry it in another boat, or pull it behind you to a spot in the marsh. Then you'd get in this and paddle off with a handful of decoys and go huntin'."

By now I am realizing a surprisingly large percentage of boats are built to go on the backs of other boats. Reed's hunting boat would certainly fit inside the 20-foot skiff I see out in the driveway, the magnum opus of his boat building career.

"Basically, I just took the lines of a Downeast lobster boat and re-drew them and adapted them to my needs," he says, pulling a tarp back to reveal the deck, with its wheel console set in the middle.

"It's like those guys on the Eastern Shore for all these years, building their own boats just to make a living. They didn't have the money to pay somebody else to design their boats or build their boats.

"They fished in the summertime and in the winter, if they needed a boat they had to build it."

As a guy who has bought boats and built boats, Reed says he has been able to compartmentalize the two pursuits.

"I look at it as any job," says Reed, who co-owns a Rehoboth Beach real estate company with his wife, Debbie.

Quickly, he adds, "But I'm not getting paid for this one. I like to build things. When I was young I worked as an electrician's helper and built furniture, and then started building houses.

"Whenever you accomplish something there's a sense of fulfillment, and that is a reward in itself.

"But I'll tell you what. If I could find a commercially made boat that performed like my 20-foot skiff here, I would buy it."

There's a quiet verging on libraryesque in Freddy's Barn, the former workshop of the Lewes Historical Society's longtime handyman, the late Fred Hudson. Cleared of all the clutter Fred left behind, the barn on the Society's Lewes campus is now a dedicated shipbuilder's shed.

"I think Fred would be proud," says Marcos Salaverria, director of education for the Lewes Historical Society, as we approach the low gray barn. In its 10 years of existence, the Society's wooden boat building program — created to sustain the region's long nautical history — has produced some 40 vessels. Most of them have been small boats, but in 2017 the group's replica of a Delaware Ducker — modeled after the original that sits in the Lewes museum — won the People's Choice Award at the Chesapeake Bay Maritime Museum's Small Craft Festival in St. Michael's, Maryland.

"It was quite something for a Delaware boat to win at a Maryland festival," says Salaverria, with some satisfaction.

Lewes Artisans At Work

On this day, 11 volunteers — 10 men and one woman — huddle around the hull of another large boat, a 16-foot sharpie. It's a flat-bottomed, shallow sailboat that was first developed in Connecticut during the 19th Century but, over time, became a mainstay of Chesapeake Bay oystermen.

The volunteers are painting the interior of the hull white to protect the Philippine mahogany wood from damage. The exterior will be coated with penetrating oil to preserve its natural color.

"Don't dab the paint — brush it in," Bob Kotowski, a former Newark area journalist and Philadelphia newscaster, cautions a volunteer. He showed up for the group's organizational meeting in 2009 and has been a boat builder ever since.

About nine months ago, this boat was a pile of wood. The crew, which convenes here twice a week — two or three

hours on Tuesdays and Thursdays — is not quite halfway through the project. As with the ducker, the plan is to take the sharpie to schools and events to educate people about coastal Delaware's boat building history.

To my untrained eye, this boat looks almost ready to set sail. Why is it going to take the better part of a year to finish it?

"Oh, Jeeze," sighs Kotowski, and immediately I know that was a stupid question.

"This boat is going to need ribs on the inside, something in the neighborhood of 46 of them," he explains with admirable patience. "If we put the ribs in first, then we'd have to paint around them, because we want them to keep their natural color. Then we've got to do a bazillion deck beams. We've gotta make a skeg, we gotta make a keel, we gotta make a centerboard, we gotta make the transom. And we've gotta make the mast, which is a real long process.

"So, yeah, a year is about right."

All the time he's talking with me, Kotowski's eyes dart repeatedly back to the work in progress. He clearly likes talking about boat building, but he'd rather be building than yakking.

"You're still dabbing," he finally says to a volunteer, and he's off.

I leave the cool shade of Fred's Barn and step into the hot, late-summer sun. To my right a lineup of historic houses, brought here over the years for safe keeping, stretch into the distance like a colonial Levittown. As I walk alongside the timbered frames I can still hear the fading chatter of boatbuilders' voices and the soft thumps and scraping of boatbuilders' tools.

They seem very much at home.

Capt. Douglas Messeck On The Beat

THE CRAB POT COP

After 29 years protecting fish, fowl, and furry creatures with Delaware's Fish & Wildlife Natural Resources Police, Capt. Douglas Messeck is Smoky Bear, Ranger Rick, Woodsy Owl and McGruff the Crime Dog all wrapped into one.

His most visible job stretches from from Memorial Day to Labor Day, when he's primarily occupied enforcing Delaware's crab pot laws.

I catch up with Messeck and his partner, Cpl. Adam Roark, just before they push off from Massey's Landing in Millsboro one morning. Of course, it doesn't much matter precisely where the pair starts their work day — there are plenty of crab pots in every finger of lower Delaware waters.

Just how many?

"A lot," says Messeck. "You should put that in all capital letters: A LOT!" So I just did.

"In Sussex County, crab pots are our number one priority. It's one of the big draws down here. Delaware is one of the few states that allow one person to use two non-commercial crab pots."

I'm not a crabber myself. Well, I crab, but not in the nautical sense. Among my major disillusionments upon moving here was discovering that crab pots are not pots at all — I'd somehow pictured big submerged cast iron cooking containers with crabs skittering in and out. Instead, they're giant cages that look a lot like Cruella de Vil's puppy crates. In any case, I've seen those cages crammed with the poor little guys, their claws stretched pitifully through the wire mesh, snapping wildly, begging me to call their immigration lawyers. Some of them clearly contain dozens of doomed crustaceans. To my untrained sensibility, two crab pots for every Delawarean seems like an awful lot.

"There are a lot of pots," Messeck agrees, "but there are also a lot of crabs. The problem is people who set their crab pot out on Sunday, then they go away until Friday, when they want to pull that pot in and eat crabs.

"But you can't leave a pot in the water for more than 72 hours. Longer than that, the crabs go through their shedding, and they get eaten by other crabs."

My eyes swell in horror.

"Plus," he adds, "small turtles can get in there and they'll drown during the week."

Now I'm shutting my eyes, but the image won't go away.

Messeck smiles reassuringly.

"It's our job to make sure that doesn't happen," he says. "So we go out on Monday, affix a crab pot sticker, and if it's still out there more than 72 hours later, we pull that pot. If you want it back, you've got to come see us and pay a fine."

Interestingly, Messeck doesn't say what happens to the confiscated crabs. I'm just going to assume they are released into the custody of their families.

Besides looking out for the crabs and turtles, Messeck and his colleagues also keep an eye out for crab pinchers. No, not crab's pinchers — people who pinch crabs.

"There are just some people who consider crab pots communal property," he says with a sigh. "So the law is you can only pull that pot if your name is on it. If your hands are on a pot and the name is not yours, and you don't have written permission, it's a violation. Crab pot tampering."

At this moment I am envisioning a new weekly *Law and Order* TV franchise: "In the nautical justice system, crustaceans are represented by two separate but equally important groups: The crab police who investigate crimes against crabs and the crabbers who pick them. These are their stories: Crab Pot Tampering — *chung-chung!*"

Every job has the go-to question people ask when they find out what you do. I work as a film critic, so I know people are always going to ask me what my favorite movie is (and I'm still trying to figure out a definitive answer). I also do travel writing, so people always wonder what's my favorite destination (in other words, where was the last place I visited?).

When you're a crab pot cop, everyone wants to know the same thing: Where's the best crabbing in Delaware.

"You know, you never know!" says Messeck, and I figure he's just punting. But he's not.

"Just last week on Love Creek, four pots contained a bushel and a half of keeper crabs. That kind of production might last two weeks, and then for the next two weeks the best crabbing might be on Indian River, then three weeks on Assawoman Bay.

"The crabs move, and you have to be there with them. The fact that there are so many crabbers and still so many crabs shows our efforts are working.

"I do wish the crabs appreciated it more, though. They keep biting us!

Not Government Issue: You Can Tell By The Period After "J"
(Photo by Carolyn Newcott)

SIGNS OF THE TIMES

There are few traffic intersections more frustrating than the one along Route 1, just north of Bethany Beach, where a truly demonic stop light is seemingly calibrated to remain green until your car — well, *my* car — is within 100 feet or so.

Inevitably that light brings me to a halt — ruining the endorphin rush of a windows-open cruise through Delaware Seashore State Park. I sit there and wait...and wait...as one or two cars come dribbling from the cross street with all the urgency of cats looking for a warm spot on a windowsill.

Thus shanghaied one recent day, I raised my eyes in frustration and found myself contemplating the sign that bears the name of that cursed cross street: Fred Hudson Road. I've always been fascinated by streets that are so specifically named. At some point someone, somewhere, was inspired to name this certain stretch of road after a particular individual, and just to make sure there would never be any confusion as to just who they had in mind, the road bears the honoree's first and last names.

So, who's Fred Hudson? After a quick Google query, I was reasonably sure our Fred Hudson was not the Canadian hockey manager Fred Hudson, part of the Kenora Thistles' 1907 Stanley Cup-winning team. Further research yielded a more likely candidate: Frederick Hudson, a longtime resident of Bishopville, Md. — just south of the Maryland-Delaware line — who died in 2008 at age 85. A World War II veteran, he was a skilled carpenter who specialized in restoring old homes.

In 1963 the then-new Lewes Historical Society hired Fred to do two weeks of work on the Burton-Ingram House, which the group had just moved from its original spot on Second Avenue to the emerging LHS complex at Shipcarpenter and Third streets. The society liked Fred's work, and perhaps more importantly, Fred liked the society: He continued to restore historic Lewes buildings for the next 40 years or more.

"They just kept finding more for me to do!" he frequently said.

As newcomers pour into coastal Delaware, the percentage of people who can look at that "Fred Hudson Road" sign and nod with recognition continues to dwindle. But the mention of Fred's name still brings a smile to the face of Rogers Jones, a former president of the Lewes Historical Society. Jones was a docent when he first met up with Fred.

"Fred was one of those iconic types of characters," recalls Jones, and he can't help but laugh a little. "If you told Fred to do something, he wouldn't do it. But if you just suggested to him that something needed to be done, it would somehow get done.

"It wasn't just carpentry. He was the maintenance and upkeep man for the society for all those years. I'm not exaggerating when I say there was nothing Fred could not do. You just couldn't tell him how to do it!"

In his later years, you'd often find Fred puttering around a small barn that's tucked into a corner of the historical society's property near downtown Lewes. Today it bears a sign: Freddie's Barn.

"Mostly, Fred worked outside that barn," says Jones. "Partly because he liked to work outside, but also because he was sort of a hoarder. It was dangerous to go in that barn. The barn had a lot of historic artifacts in it, but it was also just stuffed with what I would call a junk pile.

"One thing Fred collected in there was old wood. When he heard someone was tearing down a historic house, he'd go over and ask the owners if he could save some of the wood. Then he'd use that fine old wood for restoring other houses.

"As far as I know, the society is still using wood from Fred's collection."

You can't go around tearing up the floorboards of centuries-old houses for four decades without absorbing some of the stories behind them, and Jones says that over time Fred became something of a hoarder of historical information, too.

"Fred knew all about downtown Lewes," he says. Thoughtfully, he adds, "At least, he had lots of *stories* about downtown Lewes. I can't be sure that what he knew was the absolute truth, or just embellishment, but he could sure tell a story. Quite a character."

Jones adds that Fred was absolutely convinced several houses owned by the historical society are haunted. But that's way too good to waste in an article about street names, so we'll gather 'round the campfire for Fred's Ghost Stories some other time.

Alas, here's the thing about tracking down the origins of street names, even street names as specific as Fred Hudson Road: You can easily take a wrong turn. In my days as a cub newspaper reporter, my favorite editor made an observation that is as true today as it was 40 years ago: "The best stories too often fall prey to over-verification." And such is the case with Fred Hudson Road. After I'd put together my wonderful narrative of Fred Hudson, house rehabilitator and raconteur, I heard from Barbara Slavin, president of the Ocean View Historical Society.

"The road is named after that Fred's father," she says. "His house was on what's now Fred Hudson Road, right before you get to Coastal Highway, where the Heron Bay condos are now.

"Besides being a carpenter, he was also janitor at Lord Baltimore School."

Oddly enough, I wasn't disappointed. In trying to unravel the story behind Fred Hudson Road I'd gotten two Fred Hudsons for the price of one.

Of course, Fred Hudson Road isn't the only first-and-last name street in the area. Certainly the most-traveled one is John J Williams Highway.

It may surprise you to know that Sussex County has lots of rules regarding street names: No two roads in the same ZIP code should have similar sounding names (Beach Avenue and Beech Avenue, for instance, may not coexist); any paved road with two or more houses on it must have a street name; "avenues" generally run north and south, while "roads" head east and west.

Road names also can't have any punctuation marks, and that explains the period-less name of John J Williams Highway. Sadly, as development continues to clog this two-lane artery between Rehoboth Beach and Millsboro, I suspect thousands of drivers a day may actually curse the name of John J. Williams.

I was somewhat disappointed to learn the road is not named for John Jefferson Williams, the last soldier to die in the Civil War — unlucky enough to have been shot in a Texas skirmish a full month after Lee surrendered to Grant. As virtually every native Delawarean knows — and practically no newcomers do — John J Williams Highway is named for a beloved four-term U.S. senator who was born on a farm near Frankfort and lived in Millsboro. "Whispering Willie" got his nickname for his soft manner of speaking, but he made a whopping lot of noise in Washington as a muckraker of the first order. Corruption was a stench in Williams' nostrils, and his penchant for rooting out bad apples earned him a bunch of other nicknames, including "The Lone Wolf Investigator," "Watchdog of the Treasury," "Mr. Integrity," "Honest John" and "The Conscience of the Senate." Obviously, Williams would be woefully unqualified to hold public office today, but there were those at the time who felt Richard Nixon should have selected him to replace disgraced Spiro Agnew as his vice president.

Minos Conaway Road, a dogleg street that links Lewes Georgetown Highway with Route 1, has a lyrical name based, in part, on Greek legend. The mythical King Minos was son of Zeus and king of Crete. They say he used to feed young boys and girls to the bloodthirsty Minotaur. Locally, there have been no fewer than four generations of men named Minos Conaway over the past two centuries. Minos Talbot Connaway (1811-1894) was a farmer whose son, Minos T. Conaway (1846-1922) was a two-term representative to the Delaware General Assembly (elected nonconsecutively in 1878 and 1892). He had a son, Minos Tyndal Conaway (1895-1961) whose life was touched by tragedy: On August 15, 1944, his son, Army infantryman Minos Tee Conaway, was killed in action on the first day of the invasion of southern France. Minos Tee Conaway, who lived in Nassau, was just 24 and married, but never had a chance to have a Minos Conaway of his own.

Theodore C Freeman Highway — the stretch of road between the Cape May-Lewes Ferry and Route 1 — recently made news when the speed limit was abruptly dropped from 50 mph to 40 and a lot of surprised New Jerseyites started contributing to the Lewes municipal budget.

As a large sign by the doors to the ferry terminal relates, the road is named after an honest-to-goodness local hero: Ted Freeman, a graduate of Lewes High School, a U.S. military test pilot, an Apollo astronaut — and the first U.S. astronaut to die in the line of duty. One October day in 1964, Freeman was flying a T-38 jet trainer when he struck a goose, crippling the plane. Realizing the jet would crash into a Houston neighborhood if he bailed out, Freeman stayed with the plane until beyond the last possible moment.

All 28 surviving NASA astronauts attended Freeman's funeral — an unheard of honor. But my favorite story about him involves his burning desire to enter the U.S. Naval Academy. His grades were great, his recommendations were sterling — Sen. John J. Williams himself signed a letter — but the academy turned the Lewes farm boy down because his teeth were too crooked. Come back when your teeth are straight, and we'll take you, they said.

So young Ted enrolled in a state school for a year and underwent a torturous 12-month orthodontic regimen that at last rendered his smile worthy of a Naval Academy midshipman and future test pilot.

If he hadn't been so determined to fly, Ted Freeman could well have ended up an 89-year-old farmer today, rumbling along John J Williams Highway on his tractor, waving frustrated drivers along and smiling at them with his crooked teeth.

All Together Now: Alpacas!

SEX AND THE SINGLE ALPACA

Liz Ferguson is hoping you'll understand one important fact: They're not llamas.

"Lots of people will see our animals at a farmers market and they'll say, 'Oh, what beautiful llamas,'" says Ferguson with a semi-confused smile. "I mean, the sign says 'Alpacas'!"

I am in the driveway of the rambling home Ferguson and her husband, Jose Palma, share along a densely wooded road in Selbyville. The notion that there are alpacas somewhere around here is something I'm taking totally on faith, because from where I'm standing the only animal life in sight is a scuttling squirrel.

"Come on around back," says Liz. We turn the corner and there, standing behind a fence, is a white, long-legged critter, staring at us with soulful eyes. Its head is a ball of fluff atop a narrow stem of neck, giving the impression of a mammoth Q-tip. Most of its body has been closely cropped; the only areas clearly spared the shear are that head, a cottony tail and four fleecy legs reminiscent of fringed cowboy chaps.

"That," I think, "is the biggest poodle I've ever seen."

Only it's not a poodle; it's Navigator, one of 20 alpacas of all sizes and colors that populate the four acres of Nuevo Mundo Alpaca — "New World Alpaca" — the little ranch they and Liz and Jose call home.

We push through the gate, and immediately a number of creatures are trotting in my direction: alpacas, of course, plus a very large white dog trailed by several chickens. The alpacas seem to want me to feed them; the dog clearly wants to make sure I'm not going to hurt the alpacas; and the chickens, well, it's hard to get a read on them.

Jose Palma is Not Afraid of the Fighting Teeth

"This is Freya," says Liz, who doesn't even need to bend down to pat the massive canine's head. "She guards the alpacas against coyotes and foxes. We were surprised to find she also protects the chickens from hawks — she even scared off a bald eagle."

Which explains why the chickens are shadowing the dog.

The acreage behind the house is divided into a few large penned-in areas, spread out under a canopy of scattered trees. The animals are magnificent, even with their recently shorn coats. Alpaca fleece is among the most prized fabrics in the world: Fine and soft, the hair of a top-quality alpaca can measure as tiny as 16 microns in width — a mere wisp when compared to human hair, which comes in at a tree trunk-like 50 microns. Liz hands me a shawl made from her herd. It's dainty and light, and soft as silk. Then she shows me some work socks made of alpaca fiber — thick and robust, just the sort of sock you'd expect a lumberjack to peel off his dogs after a long day in the forest.

"It's an incredibly versatile fiber," says Liz. She sounds like an expert in all things alpaca, but she's only been at this for five years. In 2013, Liz and Jose moved here from Kentucky, where she'd raised four kids as a single mom and he'd been a manager in the retail industry. They retired to Delaware for no particular reason ("Really, it was just where the dart landed on the map," she explains) and then, while traveling in the Pacific Northwest with some friends, the couple noticed a lot of alpaca farms. "We looked at each other and said, 'Hey, that might be fun to do!'" recalls Liz. "Two weeks later we owned five alpacas."

I Want One

As they ramble about in their wide pens, the alpacas look more like Pixar characters than actual animals. I can't help but notice that they occasionally stop what they're doing to cast furtive glances at the alpacas on the other side of the fence.

And that's when Liz and Jose, like a patient mom and dad, sit me down to explain that virtually everything about raising alpacas has to do with one thing: sex. Hot, steamy, unbridled, insatiable alpaca sex.

Alpacas, it turns out, make bunny rabbits seem like Trappist monks. The males are forever on the prowl for females, ready to pull the trigger at a moment's notice. And the females, unlike most mammals, are always ready to oblige. And I mean always.

"Female alpacas ovulate on demand," says Liz with an absolutely straight face. "Seriously, they are *always* ready."

That's why the female and male alpacas have to be kept in separate stalls at all times. But even that doesn't throw cold water on the animals' amorous obsession. "A female can start ovulating just by standing next to the fence where the males are," notes Liz. "And then she just starts strutting around, teasing the bejesus out of the males. It just drives the males crazy. It's funny. And kind of cruel."

So Liz and Jose are basically custodians of a real-life Animal House, desperately trying to keep pairs from sneaking off for quickies in the hall closet. Luckily for the alpacas, Liz and Jose are also willing facilitators for their approved amorous outlets, lending males and females out to other alpaca owners looking to boost the genetic depth of their herds. Currently, four of the females here have been impregnated by lusty outsiders. Liz points out one guy, the aforementioned Navigator, who just got back from a year and a half of doing nothing but sowing his alpaca oats at a ranch.

So, as far as I can tell, alpacas live to a) be shaved once a year and b) canoodle with others of their kind year-round. For alpacas, life is good.

Jose invites me to wrap my arm around the slender neck of Tucson, a beautiful brown fellow with a mellow personality.

"He's a champion," says Liz. "He thinks he's hot stuff because he's been breeding a lot."

"Good for you, Tucson," I whisper in his twitching ear. "*Good for you!*"

"Alpacas are generally quite gentle," Liz continues. "The worst thing that happens is you might get kicked."

Kicked? I slowly pull my arm away from Tucson.

"And of course the males like Tucson here have what we call fighting teeth, in the back of their mouths. They can use those teeth to snap the tendons in another alpaca's legs or feet."

"Really?" I mouth silently.

"Yes! They can even castrate another male!"

Fascinating. I look down and realize I'm standing mere inches from Tucson's fighting teeth.

"Of course, we have the fighting teeth filed down," adds Liz, and I am slightly relieved, although even the prospect of feeling the wrath of Tucson's flattened-out fighting teeth is reason enough to step away from his business end.

In another pen, three obviously young brown alpacas try to nose their way through the fence. I ask what they're doing over there. Yep, it has to do with sex.

"That one in the middle is named Sonic Fox," says Liz. "He's too little to be in with the other males — they'll harass him and maybe even hurt him (*fighting teeth!*). But he's also old enough to impregnate somebody. So he has to be kept away from both groups. Still, you can't let an alpaca get lonely — they're very sensitive — so we borrowed those other two from another farm to keep him company."

All this sexual supervision can be taxing, but Liz and Jose are about to make their chaperone duties a bit easier: Soon they'll be herding their alpacas into trucks and taking them to a new, larger ranch in Frankford, seven miles away.

"We're building a barn big enough to keep them apart," says Liz. "There'll be two entrances. The males will go one way; the females will go another way. No more of this nonsense."

As a bonus, the larger spread — also called Nuevo Mundo Alpaca — will enable the couple to welcome the public for tours, events and, of course, merchandise sales. Liz and Jose have launched a lifestyle brand, Four Acres Living, that they hope will make alpaca-themed products a household must-have. They sell clothing, yarn, and alpaca-themed items online.

You'll also still find them selling their goods at farmers markets, usually with a couple of their four-legged associates in tow. The couple will gladly answer your questions, and they won't even mind if you call their animals llamas.

"Sometimes," Liz confides, "people ask me, 'Are those emus?' *Emus!*"

The Neighbors, At Least, Are Quiet

WHERE THE BODIES ARE BURIED

For the most part, the drivers tooling along Log Cabin Hill Road near Lewes don't notice the lady in the cemetery, but if they were to think about it, they'd realize she's out there nearly every morning.

Weather permitting, Dinah Handy-Hall will be puttering around the tombstones of Cool Spring Presbyterian Church, daintily applying cleansing solutions to the headstones of worn granite and brittle slate, lovingly placing flowers at some of the older gravesites. Sometimes her husband, Larry, will show up to help lift and reset a 200-pound monument that has tumbled due to wind or settling soil.

The rustic, rectangular church building was built in 1854, but it's the third sanctuary to stand on this site. The cemetery dates back to the 1730s — and people who lived in the same century as

William Shakespeare are among those buried there.

"I can stand at the gravesites of the McIlvanes or the Torberts," Handy-Hall says, sounding as if she's talking about the neighbors down the street, "and I know that 270 years ago their family stood at that very spot and said their farewells to their loved ones.

"Plus, the very same headstone has stood there all that time. With very minimal effort, I can extend the life of that stone by 20 years with just some water, a soft brush, and a biological cleaner."

That cleaner is a product called D-2, and it's the same stuff they use to keep the White House white.

"It's quite expensive," says Handy-Hall. "Sometimes there are stones that I have to clean as many as six times. But it works, and it doesn't damage the stone."

You would think this guardian of the cemetery must be a longtime member of Cool Spring, or at least a descendant of its occupants. But no, Handy-Hall, a retired horticulturalist and landscape designer and recent transplant from Virginia, happened to be riding her bike along Log Cabin Hill Road about 14 months ago when she noticed the place and decided it could use some attention.

"I was heartbroken, because there was so much that needed repair," she recalls. David Wall, clerk of the church session, was more than happy to let Handy-Hall — who is a member of multiple cemetery preservation groups — get to work.

"There are about 675 stones out there," she says. "I would say I've cleaned, preserved, reset or mended a third of them.

"There's lichen, algae, mold, rust — sometimes all of those things. Over time the stone can become sugary, in which case my motto is 'Do no harm.' If cleaning is going to do more harm than good, I leave it be."

Sometimes the birth and death dates carved into stones are obscured — and church lore has it that passing Civil War soldiers mischievously altered some, changing "ones" to "fours" and "sevens."

"But you can often tell the rough age of someone even if you can't find the date," says Handy-Hall. "If there's a tree [engraved] with a limb cut short, that means they died young."

The volunteer conservator can't explain her fascination with cemeteries, but it appears she was born with it.

"When I was little, I told my mother, 'When I buy a house, it's going to be next to a cemetery because I'll never have noisy neighbors.'"

The dead are underfoot all over coastal Delaware — there are some 700 identified cemeteries in Sussex County alone, according to Find a Grave, a leading web database.

For every lovingly tended church yard like Cool Spring's, there are, perhaps, dozens of small, irregularly shaped scatterings of tombstones sprouting like stone mushrooms from fields and yards, even erupting unexpectedly in dense woodlands.

The Hevalow Cemetery

Rebecca Scheck is leading me through a tight collection of trees on the outskirts of the Coastal Club development, off Beaver Dam Road near Lewes. Within sight of some handsome two-story homes, we find ourselves facing a headstone, remarkably preserved, considering our surroundings.

A small tree is growing directly in front of the stone, so you need to stand off to the side to get a good look at it. Elihu Sparrow lies under this leaf-strewn patch of woods, "At Rest" since 1928.

Nearby, a rough-hewn stone, seemingly carved freehand, marks the grave of Caleb Byrd, just 14 when he died of appendicitis, I later learn, in 1939.

"It makes me feel a little sad that they're out here like this," says Scheck, who moved here from Pennsylvania in 2018. "If you look around us, you can see these aren't the only graves out here."

Chillingly, she's right. I cast my eyes on the forest floor around me and turn 360 degrees. All around us, like indentations on a lumpy bed of leaves, shallow elongated bowls are visible in all directions. Later I'll do some cursory research online. This little patch of sacred ground is officially dubbed the Hevalow Cemetery, but also known as the Sparrow Cemetery. There are at least 37 people buried under our feet, African Americans whose birth dates reach all the way back to 1831.

The leaves and winterfall crunch beneath our feet as we head back out to the nearby street. We cross a wooden bridge, over a tributary of Goslee Creek. Then we're on Coastal Club's paved Eagle View trail, heading up an incline — toward a fenced-in, cleaned-up small cemetery in a wooded area just behind where new multi-family housing is being built.

"The hiking path used to run right through here," Scheck says, indicating the northeast side of the burial ground. "Then they realized there were bodies under there, so they moved it over."

It appears the builder has surrounded the burial site with the kind of fencing you'd use to enclose a swimming pool. The gate latch lifts easily, and we head inside.

This is the Lank Family Cemetery, the place where the longtime farmers of that name became one with the land they tilled for a century or so. Because we are almost directly across the creek from the African American Sparrow Cemetery, I can't help but wonder what the relationship was between the two families.

At first glance, the Lank graveyard seems infinitely better cared-for than the Sparrow. But Scheck, who stops by periodically to tidy things up and straighten falling stones, points out a large animal burrow excavated into the sinking grave of "Mary, Wife of

William Link," who died in 1887.

"There are foxes here," she says matter-of-factly. "Sometimes things get dug up. They once had some trouble with grave robbers. I found the heel of a shoe over there, by the fence, a week or so ago. And then, there's this…"

Scheck squats down and moves three red bricks from a small hole. Beneath them, pitted by the elements and a shade redder than the dead leaves surrounding it, lies a long, thick, intact bone.

"I think it's human," she says. "I think it's a humerus bone, the one that goes from your shoulder to your elbow."

We stare at the thing. I can't help but wonder who among the people we're six feet above is missing that bone — and how many more parts of them are scattered in the woods around us. The *beep-beep-beep* of a backing forklift floats across the narrow field separating us from the construction.

Scheck, a former art student who ended up working for the phone company her whole life, is philosophical.

"It's just a reminder," she says, carefully placing the bricks back on top of the bone. "Our body is just a suit of clothes to hold on to your soul.

"Or your innards, depending on how you want to look at it."

One thing I discovered: Property developers like to talk about cemeteries the way restaurant chefs like to talk about *e-coli*. Curious about how they handle the discovery of burial grounds right where, for instance, the clubhouse is supposed to go, I contacted five major local companies. The result: I was ghosted like the AV nerd trying to score a prom date with the homecoming queen.

"That does not surprise me," says Edward Otter, a Salisbury, Md.-based archaeologist/anthropologist who is the go-to guy when it comes to excavating cemeteries on the Delmarva Peninsula.

"What they do is they call me. They hire me to go out and delineate the cemetery, mark its boundaries so they won't dig up any bodies when they start moving dirt.

"I've done dozens of cemeteries over the years where the

developers know they've got one, but they don't know how big it is. There's always more graves than there are tombstones.

"Overall, developers are pretty good at checking things out."

I am surprised — though I suppose I shouldn't be — that he knows all about the Sparrow Cemetery.

"African American cemeteries are very often unmarked," he says. "If you look closely there, you'll find little pieces of building materials and conch shells that were used to mark graves."

The Lank Cemetery

Otter is one of those lucky people who get make a career doing precisely what they love to do: He says he's been digging up bones ever since he was a kid. But a shocking number of folks are out there right now picking through gravesites for decidedly non-historical purposes, and it appears grave robbing is not a crime high on law enforcement's priority list.

"Take the Lank Cemetery, for instance," he says. "A couple of guys from Wilmington were actually grave robbing that, thinking they might come up with some Civil War relics. They got caught, but they only got something like a $50 fine. Another family just bulldozed a cemetery, and the cop who arrested them really wanted to prosecute them. But the state Attorney General's Office just said, 'Eh, we're not interested.'"

I tell Otter about my startling experience with that big bone in the Link Cemetery.

"More than likely, it's a deer bone," he says. "But if you send me a picture, I could tell for sure."

After our phone chat, I e-mail Otter a photo I took of Scheck, the bricks, and the bone.

"That looks like a human humerus," he responds almost immediately. "I know the Coastal Club people and will call them now."

The oldest marked grave in this area is well-known and lovingly cared for: that of Margaret Huling ("In ye 76th yeare of her age 1707") in the churchyard of St. Peter's Episcopal Church in downtown Lewes. In general, though, much of the problem with knowing where all the bodies are buried appears to be our forebears' relative comfort with the proximity of death. Whereas for the past century or so Americans have tended to segregate the dead into their own necropolises, prior to that our dearly departed seldom ventured more than a few yards from the front door.

"Cemeteries have a way of showing up when you least expect them to," says Mike DiPaolo, former longtime executive director of the Lewes Historical Society. Now he's the Delaware Community Foundation's area vice president.

"Unlike, say, up in the Northeast, there are nearly no public cemeteries here; they're mostly churchyard or family cemeteries. For one thing, the population size didn't warrant public cemeteries — and also people had their own land."

While at the historical society, DiPaolo oversaw the creation of a cemetery database, documenting every known burial ground in the area.

"Most people are respectful of the cemeteries on their property," he says. "They realize the cemetery predates them, that they're stewards of land that was occupied and tended to before their time."

I am bouncing in a golf cart across a farm field outside of Georgetown, headed in the direction of a small clump of trees a hundred yards or so away. My driver is Kate Bowski, a third-grade teacher at Milton Elementary School who owns a horse farm across the street.

"I was thinking of buying this land," she explains, "and I learned that whoever bought it would be responsible for this little cemetery." Bowski didn't buy the land. But she did adopt the cemetery.

"I blame COVID," she says. "I was stuck in the house, bored out of my mind. One day I looked across the field and saw the sun just catching the gravestones. I said to myself, 'I've got to get over there.'"

Bowski has always been a history and genealogy buff. She's traced her own family, both sides, back to the 1700s. And now she saw the names etched on those nearly forgotten tombstones as another project. She copied the names that were still legible, reached out to local history buffs, and did her own online research.

We pull up to the edge of the gnarly grove. Bowski unfolds the printout of a family tree, based on her research. It traces the lineage of Nobel and Betsey Conway, both buried on this tract, both born in the early 1800s. Other names include the Wingates and the Manships and the Lawless (or possibly Wallace) clans.

At the grove's center, marked by a telltale mound of fresh dirt, is the Lincoln Tunnel-like entrance to a fox hole. Instinctively, at this point, I begin watching my step lest I trample someone's femur. As in every cemetery I've visited, there are large stones for adults and small ones for children — far too many of those. I can't help but contemplate the inordinate amount of grief that accompanied the placing of those modest, tiny, often blank markers.

Some stones seem to be sandblasted by a century or so of prevailing winds; others are surprisingly well-preserved, possibly because they spent time flat on the ground before being re-erected.

Intriguingly, Bowski says, this cemetery is not yet included in the database of Find-a-Grave.

"I'm going to see to it that changes," she says. "I've found some descendants who died as recently as 1977, so there must still be some family around, but I can't find them. That would be really cool if I could."

I catch her gazing at the family tree she's created, and I sense there's more to this project than mere boredom.

"I do feel an attachment to things that are beyond me," she says. "I've always been fascinated with historical architecture, for instance. But this is a way to get up-close and personal.

"My family teases me. They ask me if I didn't do what I do for a living, what kind of job would I like. I tell them I'd like to work in a morgue!"

We are bounding back across the field, and I turn to take one last look at this mysterious little cemetery.

If you're driving around southern Delaware and see a grove like this one surrounded by a cleared area, it's a pretty good bet there's a cemetery in there someplace. You can close your eyes and imagine the pageant of the years: A long-ago family begins burying its dead in a field, or perhaps a clearing in the woods. Then they move on, or simply dwindle until there's no one left to bury.

With passing years, the untilled land gives rise to weeds, then trees, until nature itself begins to reclaim it all. At last, those trees reach into the ground and sky, absorbing elements of the very people sheltered in their shade.

I do not find it an unpleasant thought.

The Seer Of The Boardwalk

ZOLTAR'S FATHER

"I see you over dere!"

The booming, vaguely Eastern European voice stops me as I'm walking past Zelky's Beach Arcade Central on the Rehoboth Beach boardwalk.

I'm startled. Is someone talking to me? It is the end of the summer's season. The boardwalk is crowded, and the source of that voice is obscured behind the late-season crowd.

"Yes, you!" I turn my head toward Zelky's, aglow from inside with strobing colored lights from its banks of video games.

"Come on over," the voice commands, "and let Zoltar be sharing with you your fortune!"

Of course. It's Zoltar.

Like everyone else who lives around here, I've been accosted by the turbaned mechanical fortuneteller in the glass case countless times. Yet there's something about that voice — the cranked up bass, the push-it-to-11 volume. Every time Zoltar calls to me, I have to at least glance in his direction.

Also like almost everyone else who lives here, I'm way too cool to actually stop and put actual cash into Zoltar's money slot. It's way more "local" to stand by nonchalantly and witness the tourists as they donate their hard-earned vacation funds to the swami's cause.

"Your small payment will reap great benefits if you listen to these words of wisdom from the all-knowing Zoltar!" the Gypsy advises three giggling girls who have taken the bait.

"The best place to find a helping hand is at the end of your arm!"

Creases of puzzlement flicker across their faces.

"Yes," Zoltar continues, his mechanical mouth not even trying to sync up with his words, "you must work for happiness! So go on! Take your two hands, get some money out of your pocket, and let Zoltar tell you more!"

Savvy salesman, that Zoltar. Promise the secrets of the universe, deliver almost nothing, and then suggest the *real* truth is just another dollar away.

The kids do that thing adolescent girls do, glancing at each other with their mouths hanging open, half laughing and half hooting, crouching slightly. Then they scoot off, slowing only to *ooh* and *aah* over a little girl riding a mechanical horsey.

They also forget to pick up the little fortune card Zoltar has thoughtfully dropped into a rectangular frame near the money slot. They're clearly not coming back, so I help myself.

"Sometimes it is better," it reads, "to say too little than to say too much and regret it later." I nod and make unexpected eye contact with Zoltar the Wise.

There he sits, silently stoic in his glass cubicle (or seems to sit; his legs are invisible beneath a cut-out card table). Zoltar's mechanical eyes dart intently to and fro, his right hand passes mystically above a frosted glass ball. He is patience mechanically personified.

Until 90 seconds pass.

"I AM ZOLTAR THE GREAT GYPSY!" he suddenly booms in an eruption of self-validation. "I can see your fortune! Come see it too, no?"

Despite his know-it-all air, Zoltar has no idea how close he came to losing his spot on the Boardwalk in 2017 when the Weiner family, owners of two other Rehoboth Beach arcades, bought the former Playland arcade. Zoltar had been there since at least the early 2000s.

"We weren't going to keep him," says Matt Weiner, whose father, Chuck, opened his first boardwalk location in 1985. "We thought Zoltar was this old-fashioned thing nobody would be interested in."

But then Weiner noticed small groups gathering around the soothsayer. On days when the Central Beach Arcade was closed, visitors went to the family's other locations and asked where Zoltar was.

"People seek him out year after year," says Weiner. "We had no idea how much people love him."

Zoltar may look lonely in his solitary glass booth, but he's not alone. He's got between 2,500 and 3,000 identical brothers across the U.S. from Coney Island to the Santa Monica Pier, all speaking in the same thunderous voice, all dispensing the same universal wisdom.

And they all have the same father: a pleasant-natured man named Olaf Stanton. He owns Characters Unlimited, just outside of Las Vegas, and for his entire adult life he's been cranking out animated figures for businesses, theme parks, and boardwalk attractions.

On the day I catch Stanton by phone, he's just left his warehouse/assembly plant in Boulder City, on his way to check on some Zoltar machines he's got plying their trade along Fremont Street in downtown Vegas.

Stanton's first generation of characters weren't interactive at all — they served simply as come-ons for businesses trying to draw patrons inside.

"I had a bunch of animated characters," he says. "Sea captains, cowboys, Indians, pirates — whatever someone wanted to have as an attraction in front of their businesses

"But then some people said to me, 'Well, I don't see how this figure is going to make me any money.' So I got the idea to put my character in a box, put a quarter slot on it and charge to hear it talk and tell a little story — or tell a fortune."

First Stanton introduced Old Pappy, a grizzled miner who doubled as a fortuneteller. Next came Old Pirate, who also probed the future. Then, as Zoltar might put it, good fortune smiled upon him.

"In the late 1990s I made a character I called Swami — my version of a Gypsy fortuneteller," he says.

Everyone who saw Swami recognized him immediately. With his turban, stern face and piercing eyes, Swami bore an unmistakable resemblance to another Gypsy fortuneteller-in-a-glass-box: Zoltar, the mechanical figure who grants the wish of Tom Hanks's younger self to grow up overnight in the 1988 fantasy comedy "Big." The similarity was no accident, but Stanton stopped short of adopting Zoltar's name for fear Twentieth Century Fox, or its lawyers, would come pounding on his door.

Of course, given that Swami was virtually identical to Zoltar in every way, and since he was selling quite a few of these guys, there was still the nagging possibility that someone might accuse Stanton of copyright infringement.

But no one ever complained, and Stanton began to wonder why. On a hunch, in 2006 he looked into the status of Zoltar — and was stunned to discover that, despite the character's near-universal familiarity, no one had ever filed for a trademark on him.

Stanton quickly corrected that oversight, and today the Zoltar trademark is owned by Characters Unlimited.

Most people who revisit "Big" are surprised to discover that the movie's Zoltar doesn't speak at all. Giving voice to him was Stanton's own stroke of genius — although the voice itself belongs to an actor named Josh Harrison, who works out of Nashville. Harrison voices not only the boardwalk version of the seer, but also a Zoltar slot machine and a miniature tabletop Zoltar you can have in your home (full-size models run from $5,800 to $10,500).

Stanton's one regret is that although his company licensed Zoltar for a recent Liberty Mutual Insurance commercial, somehow Harrison did not get the voice acting gig.

"That slipped through our fingers," he says sadly. "We didn't know what they were doing."

Zoltar is far from being the only character in Stanton's stable. You can still buy Pappy and Old Pirate from him — along with the white-bearded Oracle, Wyatt Earp, and Confucius. Stanton's crew of artists also makes animated animals, Santas, and dinosaurs — and they'll even whip up a custom animated figure of anyone you ask for.

"I had this one fellow who asked me to make an animated figure of his deceased mother," he says. "One day this box turned up from him containing her clothes, her jewelry, and even her teeth.

"That's a strange story."

I would be an idiot to disagree.

Dusk is falling over the Rehoboth Beach boardwalk. The servers at Kohr Bros. are leaning on the counter, pooped after a long day. The arcade attendants are propped lazily against the doors, catching the evening's first offshore breeze.

Only Zoltar remains vigilant, sitting ramrod straight at his post.

"Come closer and listen to what Zoltar has to tell you!" he enthuses. "Dream as if you'll live forever. Live as if you'll die today!

"So go on, have fun!

"And surrender more cash for more wisdom from the Great Zoltar!"

All Aboard at the Delaware SeaSide Railroad Club

WORKING ON THEIR RAILROADS

Gary Smith's train is late. It disappeared behind a stand of spruce trees and was due to come back around the bend, near the miniature grain elevator, but it's nowhere to be seen.

"It must have fallen off the track," he muses.

"I'll take a look," offers his wife, Carol, and she's off, following the rail bed into the well-tended wilderness behind their house near Milton.

Time is of the essence, because there are actually two trains running on this track: A four-car affair pulled by a classic locomotive, and a single mail car behind a boxy, train yard engine. No one's going to get hurt should the stalled train get rear-ended, but such a mishap would definitely be bad form.

For the moment, all train activity has been ceased pending resolution of the problems down track, so I have time to walk around and admire the craftsmanship of this looping — some might say loopy — layout. Besides the hand-made trains,

Smith's miniature world is populated by dozens of little hand-made frog characters: frogs in red dresses, frogs with beards, frogs lounging in a tiny station awaiting the next train, and a very pregnant frog and her frog groom getting married outside a chapel — under the watchful eye of her rifle-toting frog daddy. Near a miniature restaurant named The Bucket of Flies, a frog sits in an open outhouse reading a Sears catalog.

Off on a side track, a froggy damsel has been tied to the rails by a masked frog villain. "That's Snidely WhipFrog and Nell," says Smith. He gestures toward a gallant-looking frog on a horse. "And that's Dudley Do-frog, coming to save her!"

Certainly, Smith has gazed at this little tableau a thousand times. But he can't help but chuckle to himself.

Gary Smith and Friends

"I taught myself animation at one point," says Smith, now retired after a career working in development finance for the state. "And from there it was just a little jump to making these little guys out of polymer clay."

Carol is back from walking the line.

"Pine needles," she says, and her husband nods. When your trains are G scale — larger than most model trains but still just about 1/19th scale — an errant pine needle can be the equivalent of a redwood lying across the tracks.

Smith fiddles with a remote control. From behind the trees, the sounds of two tiny engines filter through. The trains are running again.

We all probably know someone — and by that I mean someone way beyond the years of childhood — who is model train obsessive. You'll be visiting their home for the first time, and everything seems totally normal, and suddenly they'll pop up from their chair and say, "Hey, come on downstairs. I wanna show you my trains!"

Ducking your head as you descend the basement stairs, you find yourself a Gulliver in Lilliput, towering over a teeny landscape of plaster mountains, blinking streetlights, miniature villages — and orbiting it all, like a rattling, clattering satellite, is at least one train.

Some folks don't even consign their trains to the basement. A good friend of mine near Washington, D.C., devoted an entire bedroom of his house to an elaborate train landscape. And when I lived in Florida, another friend cut holes through the adjoining wall of his living and dining rooms so his train could chug along unimpeded up near the ceiling. We'd be sitting there eating and each time the train came through — that would be every 60 seconds or so — he'd stop chewing and watch the thing pass by, seemingly amazed at the sight.

Aside from the long-ago passenger trains that once pulled into Rehoboth Beach and the tanker train that until recently crossed the old swing bridge over the Lewes-and-Rehoboth Canal, coastal Delaware doesn't really have much of a train legacy. But that seems to be all the more reason for the area's passionate railway aficionados to have focused their attention, and lavished their love, on small-scale trains.

How many of these devotees are lurking in our area's basements? There's no way to tell for sure, but Seaside Hobbies in Ocean View sponsors an annual "Train Tour" of local enthusiasts' setups — and last year the participants numbered 35.

Unsurprisingly, it seems virtually all model train enthusiasts caught the bug when they were kids. Gary Smith's trains have been plying his backyard only since 2010, but those emotional tracks stretch all the way back to his childhood in Newark.

"As a kid I had trains, of course," he recalls as his little passenger cars pull into the station. A hidden magnet activates an onboard computer that makes it stop there for a few minutes. "It was the old father-son thing; we built what's known as an HO scale set down in the basement.

"I kept those old trains, but wherever I lived there was never room in the house to put up a train layout. Then we bought this house, and I saw a magazine article about garden trains, and I thought, 'Why not?'"

Smith decided to upsize his train set to one of the larger types, which, because of its size, is more suited to outdoor use. His original layout was a single loop around a couple of trees. Before long, though, it had exploded into a variety of circles, switches, and bridges — all within a fantasy world ruled by comical amphibians.

And sometimes real ones.

"One day I came out here and this big toad was sitting right on the tracks," says Smith. "The train would come, he'd jump off — and after the train passed he'd jump right back on again!"

Along with his characters, this hobbyist builds most of his cars from scratch. "I buy the wheels, then I build the chassis and the car from wood on top of that. I bought that nice steam engine, but I built the other one."

He removes the top of his homemade engine, revealing a surprisingly complex control board. A battery powers the wheels, a light, a soundboard and a small speaker that emits real train noises. "This'll run for about five hours on a single charge," he notes.

As fun as it is to tinker with the trains, though, Smith gets just as much pleasure creating his frog people, a concept that occurred to him while dabbling in animation. "I'll just sit there laughing as I come up with ideas for them," he says, and even now he's laughing. "Over there you can see the big old sheriff frog eating doughnuts while a bank robber runs by with all the bags of money. And there's the golfer with his clubs all bent, because he's so bad at golf, just like me!"

You don't see many people obsessing over little model planes, or cars, or buses the way train people do, and Smith thinks he knows why.

"Of course it goes back to when you were a kid," he says, gently pushing the one-car train up a hill as the wheels spin. "When you're little, everything seems so big. And you see trains, and you know they're going somewhere down those tracks, but you have no idea where.

"Model trains are a way to recapture that. And it's a feeling you want to share with your kids and grandkids."

Smith, who leaves his tracks out all winter but brings his buildings and frog people in from the cold, opens his train set to the public every few years as part of a garden tour. He's also a member of the Shoreline Garden Railroad Club, with members as far north as Dover, which each year sets up crowd-pleasing displays at the Lewes Library and Wyoming Peach Festival. The group focuses on the joys and challenges of outdoor model railroading — but to the south, I found a troupe of train lovers whose model preferences chug all over the map.

Nothing really prepares you for what you'll find behind the doors of The Delaware SeaSide Railroad Club, situated in a modest Dagsboro strip mall. Even in the vestibule, before you see anything, you hear the distinctive sounds of model trains — the whining motors, the clickety-clack of wheels, the amplified whistles. Then turn the corner into the main room and, as far as the eye can see, it's trains, trains and more trains.

And guys like Earl Michael, who helped build the sprawling layout after the club moved to this location in 2016. An earlier home, in Georgetown, burned to the ground in a devastating 2011 fire — one scorched miniature boxcar, sitting on a siding in the front-room train layout, is just about the only thing that survived.

That survivor is an O-scale car made by K-Line, just one of a dizzying alphabet of model railroad types and brands dating back more than a century. Around the club's two large rooms are representatives of most of the six common train gauges: HO (probably the most popular) and, from largest to smallest, G, O, S, N and Z. (HO falls between S and N.) The classic brand names resonate like midnight train whistles in the ears of enthusiasts: American Flyer, LGB, Bachmann and, of course, Lionel — the mid-size three-railed system that circled my own family's Christmas tree when I was young.

That's the kind of train that's currently circling a miniature Main Street near the club's entrance, looping past a train yard and through a mountain topped by a whirling scale-model wind turbine. I can't help but notice the train is really zipping along those tracks, barely staying on course as it makes the turn at one end of the layout.

"This is why they call me Fast Earl," says Michael, working a controller. "I like to make my trains go fast!" He presses a button to make the whistle sound.

"I've been a train guy since I was 8," he notes. "My dad had a royal blue American Flyer. I've still got it and it still runs. I had a 9-by-14 platform that I built myself. Twelve trains and a trolley."

I should mention here that Michael, like virtually every other person I spoke to for this story, hails from a demographic that's a healthy piece beyond 50. In fact, the club recently shaved a foot or two off the front of one of its displays so members could more easily reach the tracks running farther in.

"We're not getting any younger," says Michael.

Indeed, he says, of the club's 60 or so members, the average age is between 60 and 70. About a dozen of them show up regularly for Wednesday night work sessions, building and repairing trains and adding to the elaborate displays. Still, he's happy to report there's new blood coming down the track.

"We have junior members — maybe 14 or so — ages 12 and up," he says. And train lovers of all ages come around on weekends and the work nights just to watch and play with the trains.

"I used to come around so much they thought I was a member," says Michael. "Finally, I figured I probably just ought to join. I don't really know why I love trains so much. It's better than drugs."

He thinks a moment, then adds, "In fact, I guess it is a drug!"

We head to the back room, where a mammoth HO-scale train set encompasses a complete town with working streetlights, houses, churches and businesses — including a doughnut shop with several police cars parked out front. Along the front wooden frame are a series of buttons that control various features, like a building that seems to catch fire and start smoking. The detail of these scenes is painstaking — and I soon learn that for some club members, it's the little things that make the hobby worthwhile.

"Running the trains themselves, eh, I can take it or leave it," says club member Bob Schadewald, admiring the HO wonderland. "For me, it's all in the designing. Figuring things out. The craftsmanship. For me, a train set is never finished. There's always something to add, something to make better."

Michael has headed back to the front room, where he's got his O-scale train going full speed.

"I love this place," he says. "I've got a set at home, with S, O and HO, but it's just 4 by 8. Now, we've got one guy in this club — he's got an HO setup at home that's got 400 feet of tracks. It takes up half his basement. You really ought to check him out. His name is Joe Dougherty. They call him Doc."

I don't need to be told twice: Time for a visit to Doc's place. I nose through a quiet neighborhood in the Cripple Creek Golf & Country Club and find the home of Doc Dougherty, the retired longtime owner of a cabinet company in Dagsboro.

Dougherty greets me with a smile, then leads me through his impeccably kept garage, down a set of stairs through a wood shop stocked with finely crafted furniture he's built — and finally into one of the most expansive train layouts I've ever seen inside or outside of a museum.

So sprawling is the set — pretty much occupying all the floor space except for a narrow walkway — that the eye can't take in the whole thing at once. As I walk through the door, the spectacle begins to my immediate left with a finely detailed refinery model. From there the trains run 15 feet or so to the far wall — where a small waterfront scene depicts a freighter being unloaded — into a tunneled mountain. Making a sharp right, the tracks run six feet or so along a narrow wooded area, then turn right again to the long opposite wall, where they enter a complete town dominated by another mountain and a well-lit General Electric factory. Continuing, they pass through another wilderness, then on to the shorter wall to my right where they end up in a bustling train yard with a working roundhouse.

Dougherty started building this world in December 1990. Besides 400 feet of track, his train set has 87 switches, 300 LED lights, 350 tiny trees, and uncounted buildings, large and small.

"Under normal circumstances I can run four trains at one time by myself," he says.

Dougherty seems to sense I don't know where to look first, so he helpfully guides me around. "My father started making HO models before I was born," he says, showing me a display cabinet of hand-built cars fashioned by his dad from wood and model glue. "He gave me a set of American Flyers when I was 4. In 1957 I sold them for 50 bucks, walked into a hobby shop in north Wilmington, and I haven't stopped buying and building trains since."

Like any major infrastructure project, full-size or miniature, maintenance becomes a major consideration for model train buffs. Off to one side is a workbench where Dougherty spends hours repairing old engines and building new cars. Even lost causes can be repurposed: He took a blowtorch to a hopelessly damaged plastic tanker car to make it appear like it had imploded.

"It takes me three hours to clean the track," he says. But it's the busy work of building and sustaining the train set that most captures his imagination.

"Not to say every time I fire up a train it doesn't remind me of my dad, but I enjoy working on things," he says.

Dougherty gestures toward a fast-moving Reading Railroad train zipping by. "I built that whole thing," he says. "The engines I bought, but I wanted to make them Reading engines because my dad was from Philadelphia. So I took the shells off, painted them, made all the cars, did all the decals, put the lights in the caboose. That's the kind of thing I like to do. Each car needs to be weighted, so I make lead weights for each of them. These mountains are all made out of plaster. And I like to use card stock and pieces of old architectural models for my buildings."

He reaches under the train table and rolls out a low-lying wheeled chair, its back set in a semi-reclining position. "If I need to work on the electrical, I can sit on this and roll underneath," he explains. "My best guess is I've got over 7,000 feet of wiring down there."

We watch the trains weave through the small town, past a replica Howard Johnson's restaurant.

"Actually," he confesses. "This part bores the bejesus out of me."

Sometimes I wish I had a hobby. Like most writers, my job is also what I do for fun. Frankly, I'd rather write about someone who oil-paints, or kayaks, or spends hours placing tiny trees next to miniature railroad tracks than devote the time and effort necessary to do those things myself.

Still, watching Doc Dougherty or Gary Smith tend to their little worlds, it is impossible not to be transported back to the darkened living room of my childhood home in New Jersey. It is Christmastime, and my father's Lionel set is chugging along on its simple oval course, the train's electrical ozone smell mixing with the pine needle scent of the decorated tree at its center. I am lying on my stomach, flat on the floor, watching the cars rattle by at eye level. The tree's colored lights — the big, old kind that get hot to the touch and peel over time — reflect off the shiny tracks. The engine disappears behind the small mountain of wrapped presents my family will soon tear into with Yuletide gusto, then emerges from the other side as it begins yet another orbit.

I cannot be more than 10 years old, and I am saying to myself, "I don't think I will ever be any happier than I am at this minute."

Dale Clifton Has Found Something

THE TREASURE HUNTER

Dale Clifton is supposed to be talking with me. But he's surrounded by a bunch of kids who want to know where all his incredible stuff comes from. So I wait my turn.

I bide my time browsing the seemingly endless display cabinets of Clifton's DiscoverSea Shipwreck Museum in Fenwick Island — an immense collection of coins, plates, bottles, cutlery and everyday odds and ends from shipwrecks he explores the world over. Born and raised in Milton, about 20 miles north of here, since 1995 Clifton has welcomed thousands of visitors, free of charge, to his museum, set unobtrusively on the second floor of a modest strip mall.

When he's not here curating his collection — or gently removing centuries of mud and corrosion from new items in his glass-enclosed lab on the museum floor — Clifton is spanning the globe helping recover artifacts that reveal untold stories of the world's maritime past.

When I finally get his attention, I ask who inspired him to become a treasure hunter. Lloyd Bridges? Diver Dan?

"I blame my mother," says Clifton. "She was a school librarian in Milton, and she brought home too many books like *Treasure Island*. I went out and found my first shipwreck at age 14. It was *The Faithful Steward* that sank off Indian River Inlet in 1785. That ruined me for life!"

There are those who think of shipwreck diving solely as a quest for gold bars and valuable jewelry. But while Clifton doesn't minimize the allure of sunken treasure — something has to pay the bills — he gets the most satisfaction from glimpsing the lives of everyday people centuries ago.

"We have some impressive items, like some necklaces and broaches that were made for the queen of Spain in 1622," he says. "But for me it's the personal items — the things that can be traced back to the person who owned them. Something as simple as a spoon that had a sailor's name engraved into it so no one would steal it.

"On *The Faithful Steward* I found a gold brooch, and on the back of it was a woman's name. I tracked down the great-great-great-granddaughter of the person who lost that, and presented it to her. A couple of pieces here have thumbprints on them. You pick those up, and you're literally shaking hands with history. I don't care if I never find another coin as long as I live. It's the personal items I love."

Sometimes, those items might be a little *too* personal. In his workshop, Clifton hands me what looked like an oversized brass syringe. "Take a look at this," he says. "It's clearly a syringe, right?"

I nod tentatively, but I have a dread feeling I'm about to learn something absolutely horrible.

"It's a penis syringe!" he says triumphantly. "For treating syphilis on board ships. Looks pretty horrible, but even worse is what they put in there to fight the syphilis: a concoction of gunpowder, saltpeter, sulfur and mercury."

Gently, I hand the object back to him. He chuckles, turning it over in his hand.

"I love this stuff," he says.

A Glimmering Lighthouse Stone Above A Fireplace At The Lewes Historical Society

ROCKS OF AGES

It's the shimmer that catches your eye, that glitter-like sparkle that winks at you from a neighbor's fireplace. Or from the chimney of an old house. Or from behind the rhododendrons in a garden.

For a radius of roughly 20 miles around Lewes, little outposts of glimmering granite, a rock otherwise foreign to these parts, populate homes and businesses. The stones' points of dancing light seem to twinkle against a background of blues, reds, and grays, their patterns subtly morphing as the slanting sunlight changes its angle throughout the day.

Most likely, those stones are remnants of the Cape Henlopen Lighthouse. The towering structure stood guard at the entrance to Delaware Bay from 1765 until 1926 when suddenly, with a great crash heard only by the seagulls, the tower was no more.

In a land of sand, gravel and seashells, where most homes are made of fired brick or "stick construction," the dark granite stones of lower Delaware have tales to tell — stories of geologic upheaval, geopolitical conflict, natural disaster and innovative commerce.

John Hall's home on Gravel Hill Road in Millsboro, built in the late 1970s, is a modest ranch house. But as I enter the front door the first thing I see is the spectacular living room fireplace. Carefully pieced together in a jigsaw pattern, extending from floor to ceiling, more than 60 granite stones of varying shades frame a gas hearth. Hanging to its right is an original painting of the Cape Henlopen Lighthouse, back when it was still intact on its sandy bluff.

The stones' 15-mile journey to this spot took nearly 40 years. Hall — who has just come in from his backyard garden to show me around, explains their circuitous path: They were salvaged by Isaiah Howard, who owned a house on Savannah Road near Lewes' present-day armory. Years earlier, Howard had been a "surfman" — a rough seas rescuer in the days before the Coast Guard — stationed at Cape Henlopen. Family lore says the load was hauled out by mule and wagon.

But Howard apparently had no plans for the stones beyond bringing them home. They ended up as a rock garden in his yard.

"Then in 1972 or so," Hall says, "my mother-in-law, who was a niece of the family, handled the Howards' estate. She moved the rocks down the road to *her* rock garden! Then we moved them here when we built this house in '76.

"My father-in-law was a mason. A Lewes boy he worked with busted up the stones with a hammer and chisel to make the fireplace."

Hall's home is a mini museum in honor of the lighthouse — besides the painting he has miniature models, a large photographic poster commemorating the 50th anniversary of the Great Fall, and an 1891 letter to Isaiah Howard regarding disability payments: The life of a surfman was tough on the body.

As I leave Hall's home, I notice the glinting face of a cantaloupe-sized hunk of granite in his front garden.

"Yep," he says. "That one didn't make the cut."

For about 160 years, the Lewes area coastline was punctuated by a 69-foot-tall exclamation mark: the Cape Henlopen Lighthouse. Perched atop the cape's Great Dune, its light sat at an elevation of 170 feet, visible for more than 20 miles at sea. The light was envisioned by a group of Colonial Philadelphia merchants who grew tired of their shipments ending up on the shoals of the lower Delaware Bay. They held a lottery to raise funds, then went to work financing what would be the sixth lighthouse built in North America.

Nearly a century later, inspectors commented that the lighthouse was "well built," largely because its walls — six feet thick at the base and four feet thick at the crown — were constructed of unusually high-quality rubble: relatively small chunks of granite that had been placed into forms and bound with poured concrete.

Ordinarily, builders would use local stone for rubble, but the Cape Henlopen light's builders wanted their structure to stand up to the roughest northeaster. They contracted for granite to be brought to the site from a quarry, probably located north of Wilmington. That's where the Appalachian Piedmont yields outcroppings of Brandywine Blue Gneiss rock — notable for its embedded crystals of quartz, feldspar, and pyroxene. About 570 million years ago, those rocks were created from the lava of a massive volcano. Some 100 million years later, as continental plates collided, the rocks were pushed about 12 miles underground, where they were subjected to immeasurable pressure and heat. Finally, those same forces nudged the rocks back to the surface, dark and speckled and beautiful.

Extracting the granite from the earth was, as Colonial workers might have said, bloody hard: 1700s quarrying technology was still literally in the Stone Age. Workers may have heated the quarry's granite wall with searing fire, then splashed the rock face with cold water to create fractures. Next they would have pounded wooden wedges into the cracks and expanded the crevices by soaking the wedges with water, causing chunks of rock to fall away. Or they may have simply dropped heavy iron balls onto large granite outcroppings. In any case, the resulting rocks were absolutely random in their size and shape.

From the port of Wilmington it was a simple matter to load the granite onto boats and float it down the Delaware to Lewes. When they were unloaded, the jumble of stones resembled ship ballast, which may have led to the persistent belief that the lighthouse was made from ballast taken from merchant ships.

As sturdy as the outside of the lighthouse was, however, the inside structure was made of flammable wood — which enabled the British to nearly burn the whole place down during the War of 1812 (The lighthouse keeper had refused to sell them some of his cattle for food). Pretty soon afterward, the light was up and running again.

But the inescapable fact was, no matter what anyone did, the Cape Henlopen Lighthouse was doomed from the start.

That's because the tower was constructed on nothing more than a great big sand dune, and sand dunes, by nature, come and go. For years government engineers tried to devise ways to keep the relentless powers of nature from eroding the Great Dune, but in 1924 they declared surrender and decommissioned the lighthouse. For locals, it was the beginning of a deathwatch.

"The people around here became very protective of the lighthouse — they almost personified it," says Hazel Brittingham, a lifelong Lewes resident who was born the year after the lighthouse fell and wrote a book about it.

"They'd head out there saying, 'I just want to check up on her and see how she's doing.'"

There had not been any particularly rough weather in the days leading up to the grand finale. Just a week earlier, the local residents had stood in the lighthouse's shadow engaging in an annual Easter Monday tradition, rolling eggs down the cliff.

Still, a century and a half of storms had done their work. Let's let the Gospel writer St. Matthew take it from here as he quotes Jesus talking about the guy who built his house upon the sand:

"The rain fell, the torrents raged, and the winds blew and beat against that house, and it fell — and great was its collapse!"

At about 12:45 p.m. on Monday, April 12, a local man, his name lost to history, stood on a bridge spanning the new Lewes Canal, looking toward the lighthouse.

"He looked away for a moment," says Brittingham, "and when he looked back, he couldn't believe it. She was gone!

"One day you could stand at the Lewes Dairy, or on Lewes Beach or Rehoboth Beach, and see the lighthouse standing up there against the sky, just as it had for over 150 years.

"And the next day...nothing. It must have been very strange for them."

Spilled over the sands below and into the churning sea beyond, leading up the eroded cliff like a jumbled staircase, the guts of the Cape Henlopen Lighthouse were on nauseating display. Word spread, and soon a crowd gathered, Lilliputians picking over the bones of a fallen Gulliver.

It may have started with someone taking a small granite stone as a souvenir. Soon, wagons were showing up to tote off piles of rocks. Slowly, and then with surprising efficiency, the carcass of the lighthouse began to disappear.

One can hold only so many hunks of granite under one's arms — especially when one is also trying to trudge across a sandy beach. So larger scale transportation of granite stones from Cape Henlopen to area homes and businesses became a cottage industry. The opportunity was pretty sweet: The materials were free for the taking and all a resourceful businessperson needed was a horse-drawn cart or a new-fangled motor vehicle in which to haul them. One such entrepreneur was James Travis, a local contractor who was instrumental in scattering the remains of the Cape Henlopen Lighthouse throughout Sussex County.

"He was my grandfather," says Jack Travis, who lives in Baltimore but visits Lewes regularly to drop in on his dad. "James Travis made many, many trips hauling stones to Lewes and Rehoboth in his Model A truck, building fireplaces, mostly."

It must have taken several trips to deliver enough stones to complete an ambitious project dreamed up in the 1920s by the owners of Sandy Brae Stables, located along the newly

The Willow & Marie House

established state highway that is today's Route 1. They covered the first story of the stables' main house with hundreds of granite stones — and inside they commissioned two enormous granite fireplaces. Today, thousands of drivers zip past the place — right next to a Bob Evans restaurant — oblivious to the history behind the house, which was subsequently a funeral home, a wicker furniture store, and now the Willow Marie & Co. specialty boutique.

In fact, if you open your eyes to its presence, you'll start spotting lighthouse granite all over the place.

The red brick building at the corner of Savannah Road and Second Street in Lewes started out as a bank, then became a millinery and notions store and later a bird shop. Now it's home to the Lewes Historical Society's gift shop — and along one wall, dominating the whole place, is an especially striking fireplace of lighthouse granite. A particularly artful creation with deep, varied colors, the hearth has at its center a lovely, teardrop-shaped stone.

In the months after the fall, one pile of granite came to rest a good 10 miles due west of Cape Henlopen, along Lewes-Georgetown Highway — where a dairy farmer was building a new home. Today the house is occupied by Old Wood Delaware, where owners Mary and Marty Bueneman sell salvaged furniture and reclaimed art. Inside, among the lamps and pottery, you'll find a fine lighthouse granite fireplace — and outside are several granite pillars, some supporting the carport.

Hazel Brittingham's Class Ring, Depicting The Lighthouse, On A Piece Of Henlopen Beacon Rock

How many authentic Cape Henlopen Lighthouse granite stones are out there? No one has ever tried to count, but a recent Facebook appeal for lighthouse granite stories yielded no less than 14 reports of fireplaces, walls, bars, and stairways constructed from the rubble.

Is that even possible? Could the ruins of the Cape Henlopen Lighthouse have yielded enough stones to build fireplaces all the way from the beach to Millsboro? Or has the story become an easy, impossible-to-verify selling point for generations of real estate agents?

"Well, just look at it," says Hazel Brittingham at her dining room table, waving her hand over a photo of the fallen lighthouse, the ruins looking like the spine of a beached sea serpent.

"The walls were six feet thick at the base. It was seven stories high!"

Indeed, photos of the catastrophic aftermath offer a cutaway view of the lighthouse, revealing a cylinder solid with thousands upon thousands of granite stones. A lingering look at those images raises a question not of the fireplaces' authenticity ... but of where did the rest of the stones all go?

Also lost to the shifting sands of Cape Henlopen were the lighthouse keeper's quarters, a frame house just a few yards from the base of the tower. Brittingham pushes a photo of the lighthouse and the quarters across the table to me.

Her 91-year-old eyes don't see as well as they used to, but she has this particular photo memorized.

"You can see the man on the porch of the house," she says. "He's the lighthouse keeper, don't you think? Look closer."

I push the grainy old photo nearly to my nose.

"Can you make out a woman and a child standing there in the shadows?"

I can, just barely.

"The lighthouse keeper's wife and daughter," she suggests, and there's no reason to doubt that.

"There are people attached to that building," she says softly. "It's not just a lighthouse. It's people, too."

And that is the pulse that runs through all those fine stone fireplaces, each one burning with personal histories. It's a stream of humanity that flows from 21st century living rooms to a man with a mule cart. It runs through a keeper and his kin posing on the porch, past a stubborn lighthouse steward defying an enemy, splashing over the calloused hands of workmen prying hunks of minerals from the face of the Earth.

They are not just stones. They're rocks of ages.

Larry Hobbs is Always Board on the Job

THE BOARDWALK GUY

Rehoboth Beach got its first boardwalk in 1873. Unlike today's raised boardwalk, that one was set right on the sand, which led to frequent wash-outs and, presumably, a profile that could at times more resemble a carnival ride than a flat, foot-friendly promenade.

Street Department Foreman Larry Hobbs is the latest in a long line of folks in charge of inspecting, maintaining and replacing some 30,000 pieces of wood that stretch exactly one mile from the Henlopen Hotel to Prospect Street. Standing at the beach end of Rehoboth Avenue on this particular morning, Hobbs can see his boardwalk empire stretching in both directions, as far as the eye can see.

As if with second sight, he immediately stoops to inspect a minuscule spot of bare wood in one board, where a chunk has been broken away.

"It's funny," he says, "you really can't tell how long a board will last. They should last 10 years or more, but we replaced all the boards just six years ago and we're still putting down new ones all the time. The wood is pine, and almost the minute you put it down the salt air and the rain and the sun start working on them.

"This boardwalk looks pretty good when you see it from here, but pull up any of those boards and you'll see white mold growing on the bottom."

Years ago in Rehoboth's pre-history — which is to say before I moved here in 2013 — a section of composite boardwalk samples was installed just past the shops at the boardwalk's south end.

"You can see just by looking at them they last longer than wood," says Hobbs. "But they cost more than wood, and the fact is, when people think of a boardwalk, they want wooden boards."

That's true even though wood can often mean splinters.

"And they do get splinters!" he says. "People really should wear shoes out here!

"Every year we hear about people walking barefoot and getting splinters. It's wood, you know."

Then Hobbs winces a little, perhaps a bit reluctant to confide one of the truly dirty secrets of the boardwalk.

"There's another reason to wear your shoes on the boardwalk," he says. "People don't follow the rules about dogs."

The rule is pretty simple: No dogs on the boardwalk during the summer months.

"I've seen it myself," he recalls. "Someone's dog leaves a pile on the boardwalk. I'll say, 'Hey, clean that up!' and they just look at me and say, '*You* clean it up!' And they just keep walking. Before you know it someone's stepped in it, then it's all over the place.

"And people walk *barefoot* in that? Ugh!"

You might think being Boardwalk Boss would be one of those fun jobs that you hate to come home from. But let's face it: Jobs like that don't really exist. And Hobbs' is no exception.

"When my kids were young I used to come out here with them and play the games and eat the food," he admits.

"But not so much anymore. Now the boardwalk is kinda my office, and who wants to go to the office on their day off?

Authors Note:
You may wonder how I arrived at that cavalier estimate of how many boards are in the Rehoboth Beach boardwalk. Behold:

Calculation for Board Count:
1 Mile = 5,280 Feet
Individual Board Width: 4 inches
Boards in a Foot: 3
Boards in one row of boardwalk: 5,280 feet x 3 boards per foot = 15,840
Widest Spot on Boardwalk: 4 board lengths

For Barbara Jasinski, life is picking up

THE ROADSIDE ENVIRONMENTALIST

Do me a favor and don't run over Barbara Jasinski.

Granted, she's hard to miss. Once a week, and sometimes twice, you'll see her in her yellow safety vest, trash grabber in hand, picking up garbage for a two-mile length along Angola Beach and Angola Roads near Long Neck.

If you do the math, that means Jasinski over three years has patrolled more than 600 miles of roadside all by herself.

As I chat with her along two-lane Angola Beach road, I find myself flinching as cars zip by, each coming uncomfortably close to us. I feel like I'm going to get sucked into traffic; Jasinski seems to have developed an inner gyroscope that keeps her perfectly grounded, no matter what.

Part of that is attitude, I think. Because for Barbara Jasinski, it appears the road to happiness is littered with, well, litter.

She hasn't always been a freelance environmentalist.

"My husband Ron and I moved here from Connecticut about three years ago, and I didn't do this up there because I didn't have to!" she says.

"Delaware is the first place I've lived that has garbage like this. I couldn't believe it. I mean, sometimes I do this twice a week, and even then I walk away with four large bags, full of garbage."

This is tough meat for Delawareans, who, to be honest, often get a bit mouthy when it comes to singing the praises of their state. Jasinski never stops smiling as we chat, but I'm somehow catapulted back to third grade, when Mrs. Quinn could reduce a child to tears just by grinning accusingly in his face.

As our conversation progresses, my estimation of your average Sussex County resident's environmental standards diminishes accordingly.

"Many, many people stop and say thank you," she says. But I sense there's a "then again" coming.

"Then again," she continues, "There are the ones who actually throw stuff out their windows right in front of me, just to be mean. I don't get that. I've chased down people who've thrown something out of their trucks and made them come back and pick it up."

I consider cautioning Jasinski against such rash behavior, but I sense it would do no good.

While she's been collecting our trash, it turns out, Jasinski has been observing us.

"You do learn about people's habits," she says. "There's one guy who obviously loves Reese's Peanut Butter cups, because he spreads the wrappers all along the road." I choose not to ask how she knows this particular offender is a guy. She's almost certainly right.

"And another person is crazy about Cinnamon Buns," she continues. "Every day there are wrappers. Also, up where Angola Road meets Route 24, that's where people most often decide to throw out their losing lottery tickets and liquor bottles."

By now I'm desperate for a happy ending here. And in what can only be described as an act of mercy, Jasinski gives it to me.

"I *have* discovered that other folks are starting to follow me out here," she says. "I see them picking up trash.

"Maybe I've shamed them into it, but that's okay."

Well, it worked for Mrs. Quinn.

Walter Hopkins is on the mooove

THE DAIRY FARMER

"I am not usually in here," says Walter Hopkins. Yet he is by no means unfamiliar with these surroundings.

Hopkins is standing in a concrete pit, at eye level with the veiny, full-to-milking udders of six dairy cows standing on a ledge above him.

Each cow's udder is attached to an array of nozzles, each nozzle in turn linked by hose to a milking machine.

The mechanical sounds in this spare, gloriously smelly room remind me of the airplane engine in James Thurber's *The Secret Life of Walter Mitty*: *Ta-pocketa-pocketa-pocketa-pocketa...*

I imagine one cow turning to another and muttering, "The old man'll get us through."

"The old man," and his parents before him, have run the Lewes area dairy farm that bears their name for 80 years. As he retires from farming — and Hopkins Dairy drastically downsizes its herd while the family business widens its focus to retailing and hospitality — Hopkins is getting a bit sentimental about a vanishing lifestyle.

"I've always said dairy farming isn't a job, it's a way of life," he tells me as we amble from the milking shed to a pen rustling with three-month-old calves.

"Early on, when I was getting started and before I could hire help, I would spend 18 hours a day on the job.

"Sleeping became an art form. I even leaned how to sleep standing up. Couldn't take any days off, of course, because the cows didn't take days off. You'd have to feed them, care for them, milk them, breed them. But it was so rewarding."

We arrive at the calf pens. Several elongated heads with impossibly huge eyes push between the bars, as if in greeting. Hopkins smiles at them like a proud grandfather.

"Delivering a baby calf — bringing a new life into the world — never ceased to amaze me," he says. "Of course, now I've got a bad back because of all the calves."

Being a dairy farmer, it seems, involves a lot more than just feedin' and milkin'. There's a good measure of midwifein', too.

"I must have delivered thousands," he says. "We used to have all the pregnant cows out in that back pasture, across Dairy Farm Road near Beaver Dam. Veterinarians would come out from time to time, but most often I'd go out there and deliver the babies right in the field.

"We also used to bring in professional inseminators, but soon I learned how to do that myself, as well."

I stare at him, dumbly. Did he just say what I think he said?

"Well, yeah," he says matter-of-factly. "I was very good at it. My conception rate was excellent!"

But now all those years of birthing and milking and feeding and inseminating are nearing an end. To be sure, the big, familiar Hopkins Dairy barn will remain at the corner of Route 9 and Dairy Farm Road, and summer nights will still be alive here with the sound of families lining up at the creamery window for some of the best ice cream in Delaware. A bonus for some of us (and especially for the folks living in the thousands of new homes that seem to be pressing in on the property from all sides): The overwhelming *eau de bovine* from hundreds of dairy cows will no longer waft across the landscape on hot summer nights.

"It's funny," he says. "I tell people we've gone from milking 600 cows three times a day to milking six cows twice a day."

Hopkns has sold just about all his cows to farms in Maryland, Pennsylvania — and Upstate New York, where about 450 are going to a beautiful spread east of Lake Ontario. But most of the family's dairy property remains Farmland Preservation land.

"We'll always farm it and have some cows here," he says.

"Now I'm gonna spend a lot more time with my wife, Jenny. We're going to travel a lot.

"And, of course, we will be sure to visit the cows."

The View From The Top

LET'S GET HIGH

My first night on the Rehoboth Beach Boardwalk I thought to myself, "Wow – there sure are a lot of boats out there!"

Only later did I learn I was looking across the water at the Good Ship *State of New Jersey*. Seventeen miles away, the lights of Cape May seemed to flip on and off like a chorus line of fireflies, twinkling as the rippling waters of Delaware Bay alternately hid and revealed them.

When you've spent your formative seaside years at the Jersey Shore and Jones Beach, then lived in Santa Monica and finally Palm Beach, your expectations of an offshore view are simple: a dark, flat horizon interrupted only by the occasional fishing boat, freighter, cruise ship or (gasp) drilling platform. You don't expect to peer into the darkness and behold, like Daisy's green light in *The Great Gatsby*, signs of permanent human settlement.

With subsequent beach visits, I began noticing individual features out there. Easiest to spot was the Cape May

Lighthouse, flashing white every 15 seconds, its 165-foot-high beam reaching 28 miles before being swallowed up by the Earth's curvature. Glowing red nearby were the lights of the towering Long Range Navigation antenna mast at the Cape May Coast Guard Training Center — surely the tallest thing in New Jersey south of Atlantic City.

"Gee," I thought one day, for this is the way my brain works, "if I were at the top of that tower, I'd be able to see not just Rehoboth Beach, but way beyond it. I wonder how far I could see..."

Which naturally led to the inevitable question: "Forget Cape May — how far can I see from *here*?"

I looked north along the boardwalk and caught a glimpse of the two World War II-era watch towers on Whiskey Beach in Cape Henlopen State Park — and beyond them, the gentle rise of the Great Dune.

"Let's see what we can see from up there," I thought.

The Great Dune is a geological infant: No maps before 1831 even show it. Only when the cape's trees were cut down to build Lewes' breakwater did loose windblown sand begin piling up along the coast, building the dune with amazing speed.

At 66 feet, is the Great Dune the highest natural point on Delaware's coast? No contest. Dr. Gary Wray, co-founder of the Fort Miles Historical Association, which runs the military museum atop the Great Dune, told me something I found astounding: "Delaware is the lowest state in the country," he said.

I nodded, but secretly I was thinking: "That cannot possibly be true. I mean, look at Louisiana. A lot of that place is *below* sea level!"

So, I looked it up: Of all 54 U.S. states and territories, guess which is the lowest of the low when it comes to mean elevation? Yep. So at 66 feet high, by Delaware standards the Great Dune is akin to California's Mount Whitney.

"This is the largest dune from Maine all the way down to Jockey Ridge, North Carolina — where the Wright Brothers did their magic!" Dr. Wray said, and I'm not even going to bother fact checking that.

I stood atop the Great Dune, on the paved platform just outside the museum, and looked across the bay toward New Jersey. With binoculars, from up here I could make out the frames of lower-lying buildings. Not bad. But could I get even higher? As I walked down the hill toward the parking lot, the answer stood before me like an enormous concrete exclamation mark: Tower 7, the dune's restored World War II observation platform.

According to William Grayson's book, *Delaware's Ghost Towers*, the dune beneath Tower 7 stands 40 feet above sea level. Add 70 feet for the tower itself, and you're up to 110 feet.

This would be as good as it gets.

Dusk is fast approaching. The weather is cold and a relentless wind is whipping up the dune. But the setting sun is slanting below a level of high clouds, and those low beams are illuminating the structures across the bay, contrasting them against the darkening sky.

I park at the foot of Tower 7 and begin my ascent. I'm alone here, but the wind noisily clanks the tower's metal security door against its retaining bracket. It sounds like someone is following me up the metal stairs.

Lucky for me it's not the 1940s — in which case I'd be climbing a ladder all the way.

My head emerges at the top, and a cold rag of a wind slaps my face. The sun is just a degree or two above the horizon.

I scan the landscape below. To the south, the buildings along the Rehoboth Beach boardwalk seem positively doll house-like. To the north, one glance encompasses the now-reddening Harbor of Refuge light, just beyond the sandy tip of Cape Henlopen, and the entire Delaware breakwater, pointing like a rocky finger at the East End Lighthouse. The University of Delaware wind turbine churns silently beyond a stand of trees. On the crescent of mainland around me I spot at least seven water towers and more than twice that many antennae and cell towers.

But flat as it is, Delaware's horizon is hidden behind trees, making it difficult to judge just how far away those objects are. I turn my back to them, pull my binoculars from a shoulder bag, and train it across the water.

The sun is doing its work. The opposite shore glows pink with rich detail.

I consult a map I've brought with me (Am I the only person who still belongs to AAA for the maps?). My sweep begins where land begins: Cape May Point, 13 miles to the northeast. The beacon atop the landmark lighthouse has already blinked to life, and I can see it clearer than ever. This time, though, to its left I make out a companion tower: Another World War 2 post, like this one — 100 feet high. I can imagine a young soldier my father's age standing on this spot. He flashes light signals to that distant sentry. He waits for an answer, this same frigid wind blowing through his hair.

Wildwood, 21 Miles Away

I scan slowly to the right. The windows of Cape May's seafront hotels, 15 miles away, catch the reddening sunlight. Somewhere over there is the Grand Hotel, constructed around the shaft of yet another of these concrete observation towers, a curiosity that not even the hotel's website mentions.

An orange and white water tower tells me I've now shifted my gaze to the Cape May Coast Guard Training Station, 17 miles distant. A public information officer over there has already relayed the height of that sky-high antenna mast — 625 feet —

and pointed me to some source material relating that somehow, despite those flashing lights, a small plane managed to crash into the thing in the late 1960s.

Panning farther right, the shoreline becomes less distinct and disappears. I can tell the land is turning north, away from me. Still, I've got a clear view of the coastline's most distinctive building: the stair-stepped, 12-story Grand at Diamond Beach condominiums near Wildwood. From 19 miles away, its white exterior glows like coral.

I've often spotted the Grand from boardwalk level, but to its right something new catches my eye: Extending over the water, their bases hidden behind the horizon, rise the roller coaster and Ferris wheel on Wildwood's entertainment piers, more than 21 miles in the distance. If it were summer, I bet I could see their blinking carnival lights beckoning across the waves.

I lower my binoculars. There is nothing more to see. I'm feeling pretty good about my scouting trip. After all, from a 110-foot tower the horizon is just 13 miles distant, and I've seen things nearly twice that far away.

As I head for the spiral staircase, I catch a glimpse of the Lewes-Cape May Ferry heading out on its last run of the day — and beyond, in this cloudless quadrant of the sky, I spot something curious: a pillar of smoke, or steam, way up the river.

Excitedly (for this is the sort of thing that excites me), I orient my map with the compass app on my phone. It's unmistakable: that plume is from the Hope Creek nuclear generating station all the way up in Salem County, New Jersey.

54 miles away! I am giddy.

Suddenly, at the top of the stairs appears a young couple, dashing up to catch the last rays of sunset. Almost deliriously, I point to the distant plume and explain they're looking at something that's two-thirds of the way to Philadelphia.

They smile and gesture for me to photograph them with their phone. They seem to be honeymooners.

Also, they don't speak English.

Lewes' Movie Palace

THE MOVIE MAVEN

You can count the number of classic movies made in southern Delaware on one hand. Well, actually, less than one finger. While we can appreciate Greta Gerwig coming to town to make *The Dish And The Spoon* (2012) and Lea Thompson and Judd Nelson dropping by for *Mayor Cupcake* (2011), the fact that you've never heard of either of those films tells you just how good they were.

Despite that dearth, coastal Delaware has a rich film culture — enough movie lovers to support a long-running film festival and multiple theaters, including the much-loved Cinema Art Theatre, operated by the Rehoboth Beach Film Society (Full disclosure: I'm on the board of this august group, and not just in August, but all year round).

For more than 20 years, Sue Early has served as the Society's Executive Director. Among many other jobs, she coordinates the constantly changing independent film lineup at the Cinema Arts Theatre.

I'm seated with Early at a large conference table in the society's offices — located in a vintage house just off Ocean

Highway. I've asked her if there are any movies that she wishes, in retrospect, she had not booked. And she doesn't even have to think about it.

"*Weiner-Dog*," she says, rolling her eyes.

As background, you must understand that Weiner-Dog was a 2016 Danish import that purported to be a disarming comedy about a dachshund that, according to the official description, "passes from oddball owner to oddball owner, whose radically dysfunctional lives are all impacted by the pooch."

Sounds pretty tame, right? Unfortunately, the Danish word for "comedy" must more accurately translate into English as "hideous, eye-scratching horror."

"Some really horrible things happen to that dog," she says, her eyes wide at the memory.

"People still complain to me about it: 'Why in the world did you show *Weiner-Dog*??'"

On the other hand, while the theater's patrons were united in their hatred for *Weiner-Dog*, community bonding is largely what the organization is about.

"So many people come here from somewhere else, it's hard to find ways to bond people together," she tells me. "But independent films inspire thought and conversation. I'll see complete strangers leave a film here, start discussing it in the parking lot — and they end up going for dinner or coffee together. They become friends. Film is that kind of a catalyst."

If you press any true movie lover, they will almost certainly be able to pinpoint their first film experience. Early is no exception.

"Wow — I can tell you exactly," she says. "I was about 10, and I saw this film about a father and his son who are out on a boat, and the boy somehow gets exposed to radiation and is going to die.

"So his father does everything he can to make the boy's last months happy. He even tries to steal a wolf from a zoo, because his son wants one.

"But you know, for the life of me I can't remember the name of the movie, who was in it, or anything else about it. I've searched everywhere. People have tried to help me, and I just can't find it.

"Still, I can't forget it. I think it was the first time I was faced with the concept of death. It just goes to show the power of cinema; how after 50 years a film — one you can't even remember the name of — can have a hold on you."

Of course, I became obsessed with identifying the movie that changed Sue Early's early life. I scoured the Internet using every key word trick I knew, and found a likely suspect: *The Christmas Tree* (1969), starring William Holden and Virna Lisi. I even found Roger Ebert's review, which was not nearly as glowing as Early's.

I e-mailed Early with my findings, and she responded almost immediately.

"I can't believe you found it so quickly!" she wrote. "I'm going to see if I can find it and watch it again.

"Who knows? Maybe I'll agree with the Ebert review as an adult."

I certainly hope not.

Eric Sackett Knows the Drill

THE WELL DIGGER

There's this little white cap in my side yard that I happen to know is what they call a wellhead. At some point while my house was being built, guys showed up in a truck, punched a hole in the ground at that spot and sank a pipe until they found fresh water.

That's about all I know about the mysterious world of wells and pipes and aquifers — other than the fact that every three months I write a hefty check to a company that literally pumps its one and only product out of the ground for free.

Still, every once in awhile I see a well derrick standing on a grassy lot, and I'm intrigued with the sheer primal significance of drawing water, the basis of all life, from a hole in the ground.

When I pull up the gravel driveway of Aquatech Water Specialties near Lewes I can see that a whole drilling rig has been set up for my benefit. Most prominent is the mast, about 20 feet high, towering over the spot where a well would be drilled. Stacked nearby are a bunch of 10-foot pipe lengths which would be driven into that hole, one at a time.

The guy who'd be operating the rig is Eric Sackett. Born and raised in Lewes, Sackett was a restaurant chef when, at age 30, he switched to drilling water wells. Twenty-three years later, he's still punching holes in Delmarva.

How does a chef become a well driller?

"Happenstance!" he laughs. "I was between jobs and a guy asked me what I was doing the next day. I said, 'Nothing,' and he said, 'How would you like to drill a water well?' That was in 1997, and here I am!"

Anyone who's heard their basement sump pump click on in the middle of the night knows the water table in coastal Delaware is pretty high — so I'm surprised when Sackett tells me how deep he usually has to drill for water.

"In Eastern Sussex County well depths range from 70 to 120-130 feet," he says.

Well, that's for drinking water, right? That stuff I'm spraying on my lawn doesn't have to come from depths like that, right?

Wrong.

"A lot of people think we go to different depths for irrigation and drinking water, but actually it's the same," he says. "The water you get for irrigation is the same quality water that you drink from a domestic water well."

Soooo...if it weren't for the water company's sweetheart deal with the local government, I could just suck my drinking water from my own well?

Yes and no, says Sackett.

"You still might not want to drink from your sprinklers," he cautions. "After we drill a domestic water well we chlorinate, and irrigation wells are never chlorinated. So you're taking your chances on the water quality if you drink from an irrigation well."

No more than a mile from here, I have friends whose household wells are less than 100 feet from the brackish waters of Herring Creek. And I'm guessing there are lots of irrigation wells within shouting distance of the ocean itself. Still, Sackett says, there's a good hydrologic reason why we're not spritzing our lawns with salt water.

"We're sitting on top of an aquifer called the Columbia, which is measured in billions of cubic acres of water," he says. "So the pressure of all that fresh water holds the salt water out.

"There's no problem unless the pressure of the aquifer is low. But the aquifer is a living, breathing thing, and it does what it's going to do. So, unfortunately, there are some places around here where we're starting to see salt water intrusion."

Places like...?

"Well, in South Bowers Beach the pressure gradient is awful. South Bowers Beach is the poster child for brackish water."

Still, I doubt the South Bowers Beach Chamber of Commerce will be holding a poster contest anytime soon.

2nd Time Around At Irish Eyes

THE MUSIC MAKERS

It's Saturday night at Irish Eyes in Lewes, and 2nd Time Around has the crowd right where they want them.

As lead singer/guitarist Robbie LaBlanc, keyboardist Bob Yesbek and drummer Ken Schleifer punch their way through Van Morrison's 1970 hit "Domino," the area in front of the low stage is thick with dancers, most of whom clearly gyrated to this song when it was a newly minted hit. The young wait staffers weave deftly through the jostling throng, hoisting beers and cocktails on high, smiling gamely with each "Oops, sorry" and "Oh, excuse me."

"Roll me over, Romeo!" LaBlanc belts, and the faithful sing along, a frenzied congregation with invisible hymnbooks.

The set runs through a veritable K-Tel Records hit list: Spencer Davis Group's "I'm a Man" ... a bit of Santana ... some CCR "Travelin' Band." By the time Yesbek takes the mic to let loose with Billy Joel's "New York State of Mind," the women are hanging from their guy's necks, just like they did at the high school gym back in Bethlehem, Pa., or Rahway, N.J.

The band plays on. The crowd dances on. Everyone is, at this moment, precisely where they want to be.

Break time. Yesbek heads toward my table — maneuvering through the many well-wishers who know him best as The Rehoboth Foodie, the area's premier restaurant critic.

"It's fun, isn't it?" he asks over the din, and it matters not if he means being in the band or listening to it.

You'd think Yesbek's been doing this his entire life. Only he hasn't. In fact, before one winter night in 2018, when he nervously sat down behind his black Hammond B2 organ at The Cultured Pearl in Rehoboth Beach, then-69-year-old Yesbek hadn't set foot on a stage in front of a paying audience in about 20 years.

"I had to be dragged into that gig," he recalls. "I didn't think I was ready. But I was.

"In fact, it was like I'd waited my whole life for this."

That's a familiar refrain among those who populate coastal Delaware's growing community of musicians. Many of them spent lifetimes elsewhere pursing music as a career, playing the songs demanded by frazzled mothers of the bride or exacting corporate event organizers. Others plugged away in their basements and garages, playing for the sheer love of it after long days earning their livings in decidedly non-musical fields.

But now they are here. At the beach. Where, as we all know, people come to live the lives they've dreamed of since childhood. Where a commercial graphic artist comes to paint landscapes. Where a career proposal writer comes to compose poetry. And where a keyboardist who would rather slam a piano lid on his fingers than play "Sweet Caroline" one more time comes to play the Great American Songbook.

If Bob Yesbek's original plans had worked out, he'd probably be retired from the medical profession by now. He enrolled as a University of Maryland pre-med student —

although he was still playing with a rock band in Ocean City, Md. He'd also started a small recording studio in Kensington, not far from the U-Md. campus, where most of the now-legendary records from Washington, D.C.'s Go-Go era were recorded.

"I did okay in pre-med," he says, "but my recording studio really took off, and after two years I had to get out of medicine. I had 40 people working for me."

Despite his workload, Yesbek stubbornly kept playing with combos. He performed in various lounges in and around D.C. for some 20 years. "Strictly lounge lizard stuff," he says. "It was fun, but it wasn't always what I wanted to be playing."

Finally he walked away from it, surrendering his love of performing in favor of running a music business. For two decades, he kept that portion of his life shut away, a muffled echo in his memory. But he held onto his prized instrument, that ancient Hammond B2 organ

Then, in October 2017, Yesbek found himself at the Rehoboth Beach Jazz Festival, listening to Delaware master keyboardist Bill Dilks. Standing there, he recalls, "I said to myself, 'If they can do this, I can do this! I was kickin' ass when this guy was in diapers!'"

Yesbek is seated at his black B2 organ. With its double bank of 146 keys plus 25 foot pedals for playing bass, the thing lurks like a white-toothed monster at one end of his Rehoboth Beach area living room (against the far wall stands the polished wood case of a Leslie speaker that runs on vacuum tubes).

"After that night at the jazz festival," he says, "I came straight home and started playing my B2. And I immediately got so mad at myself. The muscle memory wasn't there.

"It turns out," he says, raising his hands, "these things get rusty very quickly."

Yesbek began rehearsing with local drummer Ken Schleifer, and by mid-January "I told Ken I felt like I could play without making a complete ass out of myself."

Still, he was surprised when Schleifer booked them, along with young sax player Cody Leavel, at The Cultured Pearl. Even though Yesbek was guaranteed a friendly audience — the place

would be packed with fans of his Rehoboth Foodie column —
he told his drummer, "We're not ready!"

Then came those first notes.

"We killed it!" he recalls, smiling broadly. "It was absolute
nirvana. To this day I can play back that Cultured Pearl gig in
my mind like it's on DVD. In full living color."

Now 2nd Time Around plays a steady schedule of gigs all
over coastal Delaware. But unlike his days in D.C., where he was
a slave to the conventions of the cocktail lounge world, Yesbek
gets to play whatever he likes. At Irish Eyes the night I listened
in, the band's playlist was vintage rock 'n' roll. Elsewhere it will
be jazz. Or blues. Or 40s pop.

The variety of venues guarantees that Yesbek and company
get their fill of playing all their favorite musical genres — a
reflection of not only the cultural diversity of coastal Delaware,
but also the welcoming ears of the people who live here.

"For one thing, I'm not paralyzed by my age — because
much to my surprise I'm often not the oldest person in the
room!" he says. "There's a sense of acceptance here, because a
lot of the people who come hear us are in our age group.

"Do any of us need this band to survive? Of course not! If
we're depending on the money from playing to get by, we're in
trouble! I like to say I'd need to play three gigs a day until 2056
in order to break even! But it doesn't matter. It's a labor of
love."

If there's an empty seat at Shrimpy's Bar & Grill near
Rehoboth Beach, it's somewhere in the kitchen. This is the
second Tuesday of the month, and the Rehoboth Beach Writers
Guild has convened for an evening of members' readings. The
themes vary from month to month, and the literary genres
range from poetry to fiction to personal memoir. But there is
always one constant: Between sets of readers, Amy Felker and
Stuart Vining take the stage to perform a song — Vining
wielding his guitar, Felker cozying up to the microphone,
closing her eyes, and singing.

"Ya give me fever when you kiss me," she breathes. *"Fever in
the mornin'/ fever all through the night..."*

Vining, a Rehoboth native, has enjoyed a long music career both as a soloist and sitting in with the likes of Roy Clark, Glen Campbell, and Bonnie Raitt. Felker has been singing in public for about 10 years. And during that time she's performed with … well, Stuart Vining.

She calls herself "the little girl from the bakery." For 30 years, Felker's Notting Hill Coffee roastery/bakery has been a fixture on Lewes' Second Street. When Felker started the business at age 22, she would have been horrified if you'd asked her to hum a tune, much less stand on stage and belt out an old standard.

"I have stage fright," she says, her legs swinging freely as she sits on a bench a few doors down from her shop. "In high school I didn't want to be a lead in the play. I was happy to be in the chorus. For me, public embarrassment is always a train wreck. But I wanted to overcome it. So when I heard my friend Mike Shockley was doing an open mic night at Irish Eyes one night back in 2010, I decided, 'Well, I'm just gonna do this and it's gonna be fun.' I think it was something I'd always wanted to do, even with the stage fright.

"I decided to do a song that anyone could follow: 'Fever.' It's a repetitive kind of song, melody-wise. And I spent a month learning it. My friends must have heard 'Fever' 3,000 times.

"The night finally came, and I went up and sang it."

As she concentrated on getting the song right, Felker had no idea how it was going over. Little did she know she was auditioning for the gig of her lifetime.

"Stuart happened to be there with Maribeth Fischer [founder of the writers guild]," she says. "They were looking for someone to sing with him at a writers guild jazz night.

"Maribeth said to him, 'There's your jazz singer!'"

The pair quickly branched out far beyond performing for friends and family. For years now, Felker and Vining have been playing at local restaurants, and they recently recorded an album.

It could only have happened here, the singer believes.

"One thing about here, it's so laid back because it's the beach," she explains. "Plus, if you take one step in any direction, you're gonna hit a musician. They're everywhere. And they're very accepting. Whether you're good, bad, or indifferent, they're like, 'Yeah! Come jam with us!'

"I feel very lucky."

Sometimes, she says, the most rewarding gigs don't pay a penny.

"Once someone told me she moved here just because she heard Stuart and me rehearsing out here on a bench," she says. "How great is that?"

At first, the chattering guests at this private party in Bethany Beach barely notice the two musicians setting up in one corner of the room — one sitting at a keyboard, the other holding a 6-foot-tall upright bass. Then, as the combo eases into a swinging rendition of "Blue Skies," the conversations drop off, one by one. In less than a minute, the universal focus of attention is those two musicians.

Their music is mesmerizing. There's something about the carefree, casual way they toss the melody to each other, how their individual lines seem to weave together, like a long aural braid.

"It's supposed to be background music," says the bassist, Jeff Cooper. But there's no ignoring the pair's artistry. And small wonder: Cooper and keyboardist Glenn Pearson have been playing together since 1968, when they were high school buddies in Washington, D.C. The pair even attended Baltimore's prestigious Peabody Conservatory together.

Cooper's growing professional reputation landed him long-term gigs at venues from the Kennedy Center to off-Broadway — but in those jobs he was always playing music that somebody put in front of him.

"D.C. is expensive, and I had to support a family, so I took every gig that came down the pike, whether I wanted it or not," he says. "I mean, how many times do I need to play 'Guys and Dolls'?"

Then the beach came calling.

"My wife and I bought our home here in 2013, and I had no intention of doing any music gigs here at all," he says. "I was still busy in D.C. and had just finished doing 'Evita' in New York. But once we got here, I began to think, 'You know, I've been doing the theater thing for so long, maybe a change of pace would be nice. Maybe I could find some restaurant or country club to play at once a week.

"Well, now I'm playing most of my music here at the beach. I'll hear that some restaurant does jazz one day a week, or a library is interested in a musical lecture. There's plenty of that to keep me busy.

"The most important thing is, now I can say, 'You know what? I appreciate the offer, but no thanks!' On the other hand, I don't really turn down much work here at the beach. The people here love the kind of music I love. And that makes it easy."

A nearly full moon hangs over the Milton Theatre, and even out on Union Street the sounds of jazz filter through the open front door. The place is packed tonight for a concert celebrating the life of the late Ken Cicerale, whose smooth saxophone and warm smile accompanied any number of southern Delaware combos over the years.

Up on the stage, musicians who shared the spotlight with Cicerale speak heartfelt words, but when they turn to their instruments, the tributes truly soar.

One by one they take their turns: I immediately recognize Jeff Cooper, Bob Yesbek and drummer Ken Schleifer. There's guitarist Paul Cullen and pianist/vocalist Eva Tooker. All of these artists played with Cicerale at some time or other, most of them fairly regularly, a testament to the rich artistic cross-pollination that helps define the music scene of the Delaware beaches.

And then there's the evening's host, Vincent Varrassi, a keyboardist/vocalist and organizer of this benefit in Cicerale's honor. The two played together as part of Varrassi's band, 5th Avenue, often on this very stage.

For nearly his entire life, Varrassi had to put music second. During three decades in New Jersey public schools, he worked full time as a social studies and special education teacher. Then he spent nine years advising special needs students at Fairleigh Dickinson University. All that time, he supplemented his teacher's income by playing and singing at weddings and occasional restaurant gigs.

"What I love is playing the Great American Songbook — Frank Sinatra, Tony Bennett," he tells me when we meet up at a Lewes coffee shop. But in New Jersey his bread and butter was weddings, requiring intimate familiarity with staples like "The Chicken Dance," "Beer Barrel Polka" and whatever the happy couple's first-dance choice happened to be.

"I was never a Top 40 kind of guy, but I played it because the job required it," Varrassi laments. "At weddings, the American Songbook was just a small portion of the evening.

"Once I was playing at a place on Staten Island. This guy came in, laid $100 on me and asked me to play 'Feelings.' So of course, I was happy to play it. The only problem was, after that he thought he owned me. So for the whole evening I had to play 'Feelings' three or four times a set."

In 2009, Varrassi hung out his shingle as a private consultant to students with learning disabilities. He moved to Milton full time in 2014 — and discovered an audience that loved the classics just as much as he did.

"I think it's very freeing," he says. "I pick and choose the things I want to do. It has to do with where I am, but also with *when* I am. I'm 71. If not now, when?"

Now, Varrassi has discovered a new way to share his talents — in a way that he's been working toward his entire life.

"I always thought I would someday merge my careers and teach music to students with learning disabilities or cognitive impairment, but I never could quite make that happen," he says. "Then, a few months ago, I was approached by someone from Autism Delaware, asking if I would teach a music class for autistic adults. Well, I wasn't sure about that. I mean, what would I do?"

He leans back and lets out a big laugh, as if he could not think of a more ridiculous question.

"We meet once a week at the Milton Public Library for an hour and 10 minutes. We're dancing! We're singing! We're clapping in time! It's fantastic! Two weeks ago I brought in a four-piece band. Next week a guy's coming in with steel drums."

His eyes are gleaming. Certainly this is better than a gig on Staten Island.

We discard our coffee cups and head for the parking lot. As we say goodbye, he stops short.

"Oh, and 'You Light Up My Life'!" he adds. "That's another song I'm glad I'll never have to sing again!"

Joe Privitcra Hangs on for Deer Life

THE TAXIDERMIST

I was hoping the Harbeson workplace of taxidermist Joe Privitcra would resemble Norman Bates' motel office in Alfred Hitchcock's *Psycho*: a shadowy, sinister, crypt-like space with menacing stuffed predators peering downward from bookcases and shelves.

Instead, I find a brightly lit garage-like room with humming freezers, a high-tech pelt drying machine, and lots of friendly looking critter heads gazing eagerly from the walls.

There are also impressive tools and plastic foam forms on which prepared animal skins are stretched.

"Sometimes the spouses of hunters don't really understand what it is I do," says Privitcra, who ran a Long Island, NY taxidermy business for nearly three decades before opening Island Outfitters Taxidermy in 2017.

"Yeah, I gotta deal with some blood when I skin the animal. That takes me about 20 minutes. You take the hide, roll it inside-out and salt it to kill the bacteria and dehydrate it. Then it's off to the tannery, and it comes back as suede.

"That's all some people want done — they'll throw the skin over a couch or make a blanket. If they want to mount it, I have these foam forms that I'll stretch the skin over."

So, no actual stuffing of animal skins. I confess to Privitcra I'm a little disappointed to hear that, but now that I think about it, everything I know about taxidermy I learned from horror movies.

"Back in the '50s, they used to actually save the deer's skull," he says, clearly trying to make me feel better.

"And when the tanned skin came back they'd use papier-mâché to build the head over the skull before stretching the skin on it. That took forever.

"But there's still some art to it. I've studied deer anatomy to make sure I get things right. For instance, before I stretch a deer skin over the form, I'll use clay to build up some subtle features."

He points to a delicate bulge beneath the eye of a deer head he's working on. "Like that long vein that extends under the deer's eye," he says. "That's the sort of thing a guy who knows his deer will appreciate."

I don't know a deer from a Dalmatian, and I'm still impressed.

"I do about 200 white tails a year," he says. "But guys also come in with foxes, otters, and beavers, turkeys and waterfowl.

"I've even done chipmunks — although basically I just send them out to get freeze dried."

Poor Alvin.

Privitcra used to mount people's dogs for them, but he found it distasteful.

"I ask people, 'Do you *really* want to see your pet sitting there forever?'"

Clearly, Norman Bates would have had to take his business elsewhere.

Cindy Stevens' Finned Friends Lurk Just Below The Surface

A FISH POOPS IN SELBYVILLE

Just below the surface, swimming in formation, the gold-hued forms of 75 enormous fish — koi, goldfish, and catfish — circle endlessly with the gentle, whirling current in an 850-gallon tub. Head to tail, fin to fin, the procession persists, silent save for the gentle gurgle of an aerator. An occasional rebel will turn and push against the flow, but the upstream battle never lasts long: The school prevails, and the clockwise course continues, day and night.

"There they are," says Cindy Stevens fondly, smiling down at her milling minions.

She tosses some lettuce pieces onto the surface, hoping one or two fish will nudge their snouts upwards so I can get a better look at them.

"Come on, babies!" she coaxes. But no one seems interested.

As the song says, fish gotta swim.

And poop. Definitely, poop. In fact, fish feces is the very reason these particular fish ply the waters of this particular tank.

"Yep," says Stevens, her gaze penetrating the water's surface. "It's alllllll about the poo."

Bearhole Farms sits near Selbyville on the south side of Bearhole Road. The road's two-word name is affirmed by the two signs at either end of its 1½-mile length, although properties here are just as likely to go with "Bear Hole" as their address. Either way, the name is a curiosity, since in all of recorded history no one in Delaware has ever seen a bear south of Wilmington.

Stevens grew up in South Bethany and moved to Washington, D.C., to become a bartender and florist (concurrently, not consecutively). But the beach kept calling her home, so she returned to open a restaurant and, 19 years ago, start Bearhole Farms, selling flowers, vegetables and local seafood. In 2015, inspired by a friend in Florida, she decided to try growing food through aquaponics — a system that uses fish waste to fertilize crops.

In spring, summer and fall, the shelters at Bearhole Farms are stocked with flowers, garden plants, and vegetables. Out back, there's a small performance stage where, even in COVID days, musicians performed for small, socially distanced audiences.

But it is wintertime during my visit, and just about the only thing growing at Bearhole Farms is the aquaponic lettuce and arugula. That's where the fish — and fish poop — come in.

Stevens leads me into a long, Quonset hut-shaped shelter sheathed in translucent plastic. From the far end, extending most of the way to the entrance, are paired lines of growing plants. Close to the ground are two rows of leaf lettuce and hybrid romaine; suspended above them are shelves of Swiss chard and arugula, all linked by PVC tubes.

And right near the doorway, big and blue, stands the fish tank. The critters are enormous — the size of French bread loaves. It's difficult, but I manage to resist telling Stevens a joke my kids and I have been sharing for 30 years:

"I saw a pond with big orange fish in it."

"Koi?"

"No, they were very friendly!"

These fish aren't just big, they're old: six years, in fact. But that's nothing.

"I've got a koi pond at my house with a fish that's 22 years old," says Stevens. "They can live up to 35 or 40 years."

Stevens's fish are of particularly hardy varieties, able to thrive in near-freezing waters.

"But we keep it at 55 or above," she says. "Any lower than that and they won't eat — so they won't poop."

So, we're back to that, and why not? Switching to a professorial mode that reminds me of my old high school science teacher, Stevens leads me along the Path of Poop, showing me how the poopy water is drawn from the main fish tank and then filtered through three more. During the process, the ammonia in the fishy feces is exposed to a bacteria called *nitrosomonas*, which converts it into a nitrite — then the nitrite is turned into nitrate, a plant nutrient, by the bacteria *nitrobacter.*

Finally, the nutrient-rich water is pumped into the lettuce and arugula beds, where the plants float on buoyant foam mats, their roots extending into the water below, sucking up the liquefied plant food as if through a tangle of straws. Besides nitrates, the plants also absorb ammonia — which they thrive on, whereas it would be poisonous for the fish. Eventually the poop-free water heads back into the main tank, where Stevens' fish are happy to start the whole process over again.

Watching the fish in their mundane routine, I can't help but feel a little sorry for them. Sure, they're fish, but even fish need something to occasionally amuse themselves, right?

As it turns out, these big fish do, indeed, enjoy one off-duty activity: making little fish. Stevens ushers me over to a fiberglass faux-rock pond, where miniature versions of the big fish swim to their hearts' content.

"We had no idea they were reproducing," says Stevens. "We figured any eggs they laid and fertilized would get filtered out in the process."

But then one day Stevens noticed the lettuce seemed to be suffering.

"We lifted the mats and found these guys, eating the roots."

Outside the shelter, Stevens indicates another tank. That's where, each day, 2 to 5 gallons of slurry — the solid leftovers of the fish poop — are pumped. But there's even a use for that.

"It's perfect for fertilizing [garden] vegetables," she says.

Gazing back at the fish-and-salad shelter, I'm reminded of that scene from "The Martian" where Matt Damon grows potatoes on the Red Planet in a flimsy structure much like this one.

"You could do this on Mars," I tell Stevens. "You'd just need to bring fish with you."

"Well," she says, "you *could* do all this with human poo. But people would freak out."

For now, the Koi have job security.

Julie Hudson Gets Her Props

THE AERODROME MANAGER

They say nothing is free these days. But if you happen to own a small airplane, you can come and go as often as you like, any time of the day or night, free of charge at the grassy expanse of Eagle Crest Aerodrome along Route 1 near Milton.

The putter of private planes has drifted through the air here since local flying legend Joe Hudson opened the place in 1952. What started as a small crop dusting business has in the ensuing decades exploded into one of the region's top real estate concerns — but at the aerodrome, Hudson's family remains committed to their aviation roots.

I'm walking across that close-cropped green field with Julie Hudson — Joe's granddaughter-in-law — who's the aerodrome manager.

Most of all, I'm intrigued with the term "aerodrome." There's a quaintness to it; like the sort of place the Red Baron would have landed his Sopwith Camel following a World War I dogfight over the farms of France. And although the term can technically be applied even to a sprawling place like JFK International Airport, it has come to mean precisely the sort of idyllic airpark I'm right now visiting.

"We're just a small airport with grass landing strips," says Hudson. Along Eagle Crest's periphery stand some large hangars, the futuristic Futuro home — and, it turns out, 27 individual houses, each with a garage wide enough to park a personal airplane inside.

"A lot of people don't realize that Eagle Crest Aerodrome is actually a fly-in community," says Hudson. "All these homes are fly-in homes. Each has its own hangar.

"We own the runway, and the homeowners handle maintenance of it. They're very hands-on. The grass gets cut twice a week, and twice a year they bring in a steamroller to roll the grass down. The homeowners take turns driving it."

But the homeowners don't have exclusive use of the airstrip.

"Anyone is welcome to land their plane or helicopter here for free," she says — but they'd better be prepared for a welcoming committee. Whenever a strange plane lands, the neighbors hop into their golf carts and head out to see what's up.

"The homeowners love it!" says Hudson. "They start asking questions: 'Who are you? Where you from? What are you doing here?'"

In fact, just about the only way to land unnoticed at Eagle Crest is to fly in at night. That's what the area's super-rich VIPs do when they want to slip unnoticed into their mini-Versailles by the sea. Or if they decide last-minute to pop down from the Hamptons for crab cakes at Woody's.

"Some fly 45 minutes just for dinner in Lewes," says Hudson. "They get picked up by limos and off they go. We never see them."

Eagle Crest's biggest to-do of recent years came just after then-former Vice President Joe Biden, who has a home in North Shores, left office following the Obama Administration.

"He flew in here with the Prince of Jordan," Hudson recalls. "The Secret Service showed up first, and they were really nice. The Prince had two men with him who just sat here all day. They didn't talk, didn't want anything to eat or drink. Polite, but I guess their job was just to sit."

I part company with Hudson just as a private helicopter is circling in for a landing. As I drive along Eagle Crest Road and then down Hudson Road, which defines the north end of the aerodrome, I catch sight of the owners' homes with their broad, low-lying garages.

It would be nice to have a garage for my airplane, I think. But then again, I'd probably just fill it up with stuff and I'd still be parking my plane out on the driveway.

Table For Two...Boo!

THE GHOSTS AT THE CAFÉ

"Thank goodness they're friendly," says Maria Fraser. "They seem playful. They seem happy."

"They" are also ghosts. Two of them, at least. And they walk the stairs and haunt the halls of Fraser's atmospheric restaurant, The Café on 26, in Ocean View.

"At first I thought I was going crazy," she adds. "It was all so...so *weird*."

As Fraser regales me with creepy tales of apparitions and disembodied late-night mayhem at her award-winning restaurant, I search her eyes for hints of hucksterism. I spent 10 years suspending disbelief reporting hokey ghost stories for the *National Enquirer*. As a writer at *National Geographic* I personally scoured the windowless rooms of the Tower of London for spirits in the middle of the night — and called out my guide when she tried to fake some rattling dishware. I think

I know a phony phantom sighter when I see one. And right now I'm not seeing one.

It is morning at the café, a lovingly restored 1920s house on busy Atlantic Avenue. The lights have not yet been turned on, and as Fraser shows me around the home's shadowy former front parlor it's not hard to imagine life here nearly 100 years ago: the original owners, Cecile Long Steele and her husband David, lounging in the love seats and snuggling on the settee.

You may not know the name Cecile Long Steele, but you have certainly seen her monuments — the miles of chicken barns that span Southern Delaware and Maryland. Even as the region's population explodes, chickens still outnumber humans here 300 to 1, and it's all thanks to Cecile, who did more to promote chicken consumption in America than Colonel Sanders and Frank Perdue put together.

In 1923 Cecile, the wife of a Bethany Beach Coast Guardsman, decided to stretch the family budget by ordering 50 chicks from a Dagsboro supplier. She planned to sell the eggs. Somewhere, somehow, an extra zero got added to the order, and a truck arrived with 500 chirping chicks.

No problem, said Cecile, just leave 'em all here.

History is silent as to what inspired Cecile to keep the flock, but it's clear that from the start she planned to sell them for broiling — a use that, strange as it seems, was utterly foreign to most people at the time. Chickens were for egg-laying, not eating — and they were killed and cooked only when their egg-laying days were over.

Cecile got her husband to build a chicken coop out back, the first "broiler house" in the state (you can still visit it at the University of Delaware Agriculture Experiment Station in Georgetown). Within weeks, Cecile's chicks had grown plump and juicy. She sold 387 of them for 67 cents a pound. The next year she raised 1,000 chickens, and the year after that 10,000. Today the tens of thousands of people who produce 200 million broiler chickens a year in Sussex County alone owe their livelihoods to the red-haired chicken lady from Ocean Ridge.

If none of this sounds like a ghost story (other than the ghosts of all those chickens), that's because we have not yet

gotten to the fateful day in 1940 when Cecilia and David —
their nest thoroughly feathered by their chicken fortune —
went for a cruise on their $10,000 yacht, *Lure*. That afternoon,
just off Ocean City, the boat exploded in a ferocious fireball. The
couple died in the water, both 40 years old.

The little town of Ocean View fell into deep mourning.
Reports say their bodies lay in state in the parlor of their home,
and local school children lined up outside to pay their respects.
Cecilia and David's bodies were buried at the Mariners Bethel
United Methodist Church Cemetery.

But their spirits, well, that's another story.

"I opened the restaurant in 2011," says Fraser. "And it was
about a year and a half before I noticed anything...*strange*."

The paper towels were first. Fraser had installed an electric
eye dispenser in each restroom; the kind that rolls out a sheet
or two with the wave of your hand.

"I'd arrive in the morning and find a ribbon of paper towel
stretching from the dispenser to the opposite wall," she says.
"At first I figured it was a malfunction. But then I thought, 'Well,
how the heck did the paper get stretched all the way across the
room?'"

It happened so often she finally gave up on the automatic
dispensers and replaced them with old-fashioned manual ones.

Not long after that Fraser arrived at the restaurant to the
sound of running water.

"I thought, 'Great! A broken pipe!' I ran upstairs and found
the water running. But not just from one faucet — from every
faucet on the second floor.

"I thought, 'Okay, this is getting creepy.'"

Weird things started happening in the kitchen. Most
memorably, an entire set of ladles flew off their rack and
clattered to the floor.

"So, I got used to the idea that we had ghosts here," she said.
"As long as my sous chef and I could keep cleaning up after
them, it wasn't so bad."

Then came the apparitions.

"I think that's what freaked me out the most," says Fraser.

There's a staircase at Café on 26 that leads from the first floor dining room to the second, where two bedrooms have been converted into another dining room and a wine room. One morning Fraser looked up the stairs — and caught sight of a woman passing across the top landing, as if going from the old bathroom to the master bedroom.

"She was wearing a long, white dress, like women wore in the 1920s," she said. "And she had long hair. She wasn't fuzzy or transparent or anything like that. She seemed solid. So I assumed it was a person. I started yelling, 'Excuse me! Excuse me can I help you?' I went upstairs, and she was nowhere. Just nowhere."

Oh, yeah — at this point, Fraser had also never heard of Cecilia Long Steele. Only after doing some research on the house did she begin to link her Lady On The Landing to coastal Delaware's Chicken Queen.

Years went by, and the sightings continued. One day Fraser watched as the woman in the white dress ascended the stairs. And before opening another morning, she caught sight of a man in a black suit pushing open the swinging kitchen door and striding toward the old parlor.

"They don't scare me anymore," she says. "Although I'll still scream if they surprise me. When I go upstairs I shout, 'I'm coming up! Don't scare me!'

"In fact, I guess I talk to them all the time. The staff has gotten used to it. I asked the ghosts to stop running the water. I said, 'It's not well water like when you lived here; it's City of Ocean View water. I'm paying for that.' And it stopped!"

So far, the ghosts of Café on 26 have never rattled a diner. But every once in awhile, while working in the kitchen, a server tells Fraser a guest absolutely insists on speaking with her. Almost always, she knows exactly what's coming.

"It will be someone who's a medium, or who's somehow psychic," she says. "They'll say, 'Do you know there are spirits present in this house?' And I'll say, 'Yeah, I know that.'

"One time a guest asked if I'd like her to describe the spirits to me. I said, 'Sure.' She told me one of them was a woman with long hair in a white dress, and the other was a man in a suit.

"I said, 'Oh yeah, I know them.'"

Another diner told Fraser the spirits wanted her to know they are pleased with how she's taking care of their old house — and especially the grounds outside. She's also gotten more temporal confirmation of that, as well.

"The grandchildren of Cecile and David still come here," she said. "They remember how David loved to take care of the yard. They said he used to go out there and pick every single dandelion, one by one."

She glances out the window, at the shady lawn where Cecile's first chicken coop once stood.

"I'm glad he's happy with the yard," she sighs, "but I draw the line at picking dandelions."

Paul Yeager in Heaven

ROLL-UP RETREATS

"Let's go visit my motorcycle," says my brother-in-law Paul Yeager, rising from a comfy chair in his living room.

I jump to my feet excitedly, because Paul Yeager's garage, attached to his house just off Minos Conaway Road near Lewes, is one of my favorite places in coastal Delaware.

Even before Yeager opens the door, I can hear music filtering from beyond it — a 24-hour symphony of sound specially selected to serenade the countless motorcycle-and-classic-car ephemera that line the shelves, walls, floor and, yes, ceiling of his positively spotless two-car garage.

On the far wall hangs a shrine to Steve McQueen — including a poster of the star preparing to make that iconic cycle jump in "The Great Escape." The steering wheel of a Triumph is mounted nearby. The industrial-grade metal cabinets above the uber-organized workbench are peppered with photos of vintage cars.

"I have a talent," he tells me, "for taking a wall and covering it with stuff."

And there in a place of honor, preening like a show dog in front of a curtain of vintage leather jackets, is Yeager's motorcycle. Not a Harley, not a Yamaha, but a Russian Ural cycle. He bought the thing new 12 years ago and has ever since been obsessively retrofitting it to resemble a standard-issue 1941 Soviet Army cycle. You might have seen a photo of him on this cycle last year in the local paper, taken during a military reenactment held at Fort Miles on Cape Henlopen. There he was, proudly astride the Ural in full Russian military regalia, seemingly just returned to Leningrad from a tour in the Balkans. The bike has a fully functional side car on which Yeager has mounted a genuine Russian machine gun. The barrel is filled with lead to render it inoperable, but that doesn't stop the occasional cop from pulling him over to check it out. My sister-in-law Emily, Paul's wife, looks adorable in the side car, but it is really meant to be occupied by a beady-eyed, square-jawed Soviet-era conscript, squinting through the sights and keeping watch for snipers.

I've known lots of people who love their motorcycles, but Yeager is the only guy I know whose motorcycle probably loves him back. After all, with custom lighting, a separate HVAC system — set to 69 degrees year-round — and constant mood music punctuated by the occasional sounds of revving Alfa Romeos and Ferraris, the Ural enjoys the kind of pampered suburban luxury most of our parents could only have dreamed of providing for us.

It was after a recent visit to the Yeager place that I began paying attention to the occasional open garages that yawn upon the streets and back roads of coastal Delaware. Most of them, of course, are like mine — utilitarian homes for one or two cars. Either that, or the space has been commandeered by all the stuff that couldn't fit into the new house when the owner moved here. Mine is an unpainted space with one bare bulb and heavy-duty wood shelving, a parking area my wife Carolyn's orange 30th anniversary Mazda Miata hardtop convertible reluctantly shares with my black 2016 Honda Civic.

But the more I looked, the more I caught glimpses of garages that hold more than vehicles, tools and half-empty paint cans. I discovered a subculture of semi-sacred spaces; sanctuaries where — away from the requisite matched couches and ottomans, "Life's a Beach" wall hangings and TVs mounted atop fireplaces — life's true passions can be pursued within the confines of three walls and an overhead door.

A time/space vortex has been whirling just north of the railroad tracks in Lewes ever since Barry Sipple and Anita Naylor bought their place three years ago. The chronological slip begins right there on the sidewalk outside the couple's garage, where an ancient Texaco gas pump seems poised to dispense fuel for an advertised 15½ cents per gallon — and at any second you expect the old-timey red ECO Tireflator air pump to start hissing and dinging. For good measure, there's a 1972 Volkswagen "Bay Window" van parked parallel to the garage door — which Sipple rolls up to reveal a green, somewhat worn, 1971 Volkswagen Beetle he and Naylor are restoring. I can't help but notice it's a twin to the one once owned by my big brother, Ed — a car we once drove through the streets of Manhattan with a snapped clutch cable.

"Make sure you get a picture of the back window," Sipple tells me. In the accumulating dust someone has used a finger to etch a peace symbol.

"People stop all the time to look at the bus," says Sipple, who's retired after running a used-car business in Laurel for most of his life. Climbing in, he closes the door. Instead of the substantial "thud" that is now engineered into even small cars, I hear the familiar, tinny VW van door sound — oddly reminiscent of a loosely hung screen slapping shut.

"One guy came back with a picture of himself sitting on top of his VW bus at Woodstock," he says. "Pretty cool. This is probably my seventh VW bus. I used to be able to buy one for $2,500, put

$2,500 into it, drive it for five years and then sell it for five grand. But now they're really expensive."

Sipple and Naylor — who both grew up in Smyrna and went to high school together — recently finished renovating the house. They have now turned their attention to the garage. Already, the pegboard walls are lined with shelves of cast metal model cars

Barry Sipple and Anita Naylor in Their Bus

dating back to the 1940s. On the highest shelf is the oldest: a heavy-looking pressed-steel tow truck made by Wyandotte, a beloved toy company that specialized in metal toys and went bankrupt when plastic became the rage. A collection of antique oil cans sits atop a tool cabinet.

Sipple started collecting car paraphernalia when he was working in the accounting department of a car dealership. When the business would throw away, say, a fine old metal windshield wiper supply box, he'd rescue it from the trash and bring it home.

"It's easy to collect a lot of that stuff when you're in the car business," says Naylor, who's retired after a career at Lockheed Martin. "And this garage seemed like a really good place for it all to live."

"I guess I'm not in the car business anymore," adds her husband, "but the car business is sort of in me. I come out here and work on this VW, surrounded by this stuff, and I feel at home."

I bid adieu to the 1950s idyll of Sipple and Naylor's garage and head back toward my car, parked on Railroad Avenue. Just a couple of houses down, I stop in my tracks. At the top of a short driveway, behind the proscenium of an open double garage door, is what appears to be a small Broadway stage complete with a rich velvet curtain. It's pulled back to reveal an enormous vintage theater poster for Walt Disney's "Cinderella." Hanging on the side walls are scores of signed posters for Broadway shows old and new, immortal and less so.

As one who easily forgets the boundaries of polite society, I immediately venture up the drive and tentatively poke my head through the garage door. As my eyes adapt to the relative darkness inside, I am aware of the sound of a car pulling in behind me. It's a situation I find myself in quite often: The writer in me frequently adopts a trespass-first/answer-questions-later attitude. But as is usually the case, the driver of the car pops out smiling, clearly pleased that someone has taken notice of his personal passion.

The owner of this Broadway-on-the-Broadkill is Jim Ryan, a onetime child actor and lifelong theater lover who has semi-retired to Lewes after a career as a major event organizer. He's run inaugural balls for Ronald Reagan and Bill Clinton, organized conventions for thousands in Las Vegas — and now operates a scaled-back event business from a little office in his house.

"People come up here all the time," he says. "They ask about the stuff; they ask about the art."

Ryan stands proudly in the middle of his theatrical garage, lingering under a full-size disco ball that's hung from the ceiling — along with a high school marching band uniform and an Uncle

Sam suit — and gestures toward the array of posters on one wall.

"About half of these are mine, and the rest were given to me by a friend," he says. "Here's 'Hello, Dolly!,' signed by Pearl Bailey and Cab Calloway. Look at that one from 'How to Succeed in Business Without Really Trying' — signed by Rudy Vallee and Robert Morse."

Above the garage door, the faces of Broadway immortals gaze down on us from an array of Playbill covers, as if occupying an all-star mezzanine.

"I've got about 150 more of those," he says. "I think I'll have to put them on the ceiling. I have to figure out how to do that. I'll be on my back, like Michelangelo."

Glancing at me, Ryan seems a tad embarrassed.

"It's not that I'm a hoarder," he says, "but I don't believe in putting stuff in drawers."

When Ryan entertains guests, the garage becomes a focus of post-dinner activity: cigars are broken out, packs of cards are opened.

"Some people say, 'Why do you have all this stuff out here in your garage? It's not even part of the house, really.' But you'd be surprised how much time you spend in your garage. I'm out here four or five times a day. Why shouldn't I enjoy it?"

Just one thing confuses me. Personal passions aside, garages still serve an essential household function: They are where we put all our ugly stuff, like paint cans and cleaning fluids.

"Ah!" says Ryan triumphantly. "That's the genius of the red velvet curtain." He pulls it back — and reveals shelves of unsightly household odds and ends.

He smiles. "You might say it's all backstage."

"I've got to warn you," says Linn Worrell. "The garage is a mess!" And then he opens the door on the most pristine, utterly organized garage I have ever laid eyes on.

A retired operations supervisor for petroleum companies, Worrell now spends much of his spare time doing woodwork here in his garage. There are two or three heavy-duty wood cutting and shaping machines lined along one wall, but Worrell uses them sparingly — just long enough to get his wood pieces whittled down to the right size for making intricate, delicate pieces of woodworker's art.

"It's the hand tools that I love," he says. "It's relaxing, and most of all it's nearly noiseless. And that's a nice escape in a noisy world."

He's especially fond of building wooden lap desks in the style of the Shakers, a project that generally takes about two weeks. But now he's making plans to embark on creating the lap desk lover's Holy Grail: a reproduction of Thomas Jefferson's portable writing desk, a painstakingly elaborate affair with drawers, inkwells, dovetailed pieces and adjustable levels.

"It might take me 10 years," he shrugs.

If so, he'll spend that decade in style. The garage's patterned gray, black and blue floor is made of RaceDeck, a plastic tile with a Lego-like bottom that's durable, easily cleaned, and comfortable to stand on. Tools are hung — perfectly parallel or perpendicular to the floor — on white peg boards. To one side stands a lovingly built small pine cabinet with dainty drawers. Boards stand at attention, filed according to height and project, in neat groupings against the wall. Light pours in through two large windows that illuminate Worrell's work space — a sturdy wooden table made of knot-free European birch. Positioned as it is in the corner of the garage beneath the two windows, it more resembles an executive's office desk than a craftsman's workbench.

Most importantly, behind the bench is a comfy office chair, perfect for settling in for detailed wood work.

"He's so patient," says Worrell's wife of 51 years, Margie, a retired schoolteacher. "He just keeps working on those tiny little joints over and over until they're perfect. If it were me I'd be snapping the pieces of wood in frustration, but he just keeps at it.

"The irony is, he never was a really patient person when we got married. That's the weird part."

"It's the working on a project that I love," he explains. "I tend to give things away when I finish with them. I built a workbench before this one, then I gave it away. And when I finish the Thomas Jefferson writing desk, I'm giving that to our neighbor."

Worrell turns on the radio that accompanies his hours alone in his garage. Soon the space is filled with the sound of Lloyd Price singing the 1950s hit "Personality."

He pulls out the plans for the Jefferson desk and can't help but smile a little. This will be 10 years well spent.

Driving back home, I think about one particular corner of Paul Yeager's garage — a gallery of small black-and-white photos. They are of a dilapidated old garage in Pittsburgh, the one where he grew up working on cars and hanging out with his brothers.

"It had a dirt and cinder floor — we changed engines in there," recalled Yeager, who spent his career as an orientation and mobility specialist for the visually impaired. "When I was in graduate school I had an old garage that leaked rain on my Datsun. Later I had a garage that got so cold in the winter I had to put electric blankets over my two motorcycles to protect the oil.

"So I always had this dream that someday, when I retired, my home would have a real comfortable garage with the things I want in it. And to be honest, this garage is one of the reasons we bought this house.

"It goes back to my father, and to my brothers and to the time we spent together working on cars. This place is so different from what we had, but it makes me feel close to them."

I pull my Honda Civic into my driveway. The garage door rolls up and there's Carolyn's orange Miata, its downturned headlights frowning disapprovingly. Gingerly, I open the Civic's door, ever so careful not to let it touch the Miata's unblemished paint job.

Emerging from my car, I cast my gaze along the industrial-strength shelves we have built to hold all the things that would not fit in our house. There are the blow-up beach toys we pull down when the grandchildren visit. Tucked off to one side is a signed Robert Redford movie poster that's just too big for any of our walls. Up ahead is a neat lineup of Tupperware bins containing the photo albums, documents, and memorabilia each of us brought to our marriage nine years ago. On a shelf to my right sits a plush battery-operated figure of the least popular "Star Wars" character, Jar-Jar Binks, banished to the garage because he insists, with complete randomness, on occasionally shaking wildly and exclaiming, "Meesa Wuv You!!"

I must admit I've been a little jealous of the dedicated garage curators I've been meeting. Their garages are so thought-out ... so defined ... so *them*.

But standing here, trying not to smudge the Miata, I'm beginning to feel a little better. A lot better, in fact. This is my garage. And it's me.

Lister & Vos; Buddy Cops

THE K-9 TEAM

Spend five minutes with Delaware State Parks Officer John Lister and his partner, a 3-year-old Belgian Malinois named Vos, and you wonder how long it will take for someone to build a reality TV show around them.

I mean, here's Lister, handsome and fit in his uniform, complete with a boyish, dimpled smile, and here's Vos, striking and devoted, with the friendly personality of a no-nonsense puppy.

Vos resembles a smaller German shepherd — indeed, some people call the breed Belgian shepherds, which encapsulates that subliminal distinction we've always made about Germans and Belgians: You want a German to build the police car, but you're prefer the cop inside to be Belgian.

I meet up with Lister and Vos (man, it even *sounds* like a TV show) outside their headquarters at Henlopen State Park.

The two have been paired up for eight months, ever since they met at police dog school.

"We're buddies," says Lister. "They showed us 22 dogs, and I was interested in Vos the moment I saw him.

"I liked his demeanor. He had a different name, but I named him Vos — Dutch for fox — because he's red and black like a fox and he's Belgian. He's very social — little kids sense that and run up to play with him. That's okay, but I try to keep him social without expecting a belly rub from everybody."

It must be hard, I suggest, for Lister not to think of Vos as his dog. And Lister looks at me like I'm crazy.

"He *is* my dog!" he says. "He lives with me. We spend all our time together. And when he retires, after seven or eight years, he'll stay with me. But unlike most people, he won't have to retire to the beach. He's already here!"

Like all police dogs, Vos had a "major" in police dog school: He's certified in human scent tracking.

"That comes in handy here in the park, finding lost children who might have wandered away, or adults with dementia," says Lister.

Now, this is exciting, I think. I immediately envision Lister holding a child's shirt up to Vos' nose and shouting, "Go find 'em, boy!"

"Ah, no," Lister says, bursting my thought balloon. "We don't usually do that thing you see on TV. I just take Vos to the place the missing person was last seen and give him his track command."

I think Lister can sense my disappointment.

"Of course, he also knows how to track down people who are running away from us," he offers, and I perk up. "In fact, we were out until 4 this morning on a drug arrest case. Later this year, Vos will get trained in narcotics tracking.

"It's not like we're in Detroit, but everyone likes to go on vacation. Even criminals."

That reality series can't start a moment too soon. Now he's even writing the script.

St. George's Chapel

GOIN' TO THE CHAPELS

Red balloons reach for the ceiling of Indian Mission United Methodist Church, each one tethered by ribbon to the end of a pew. They sway to and fro, gently buffeted by whispery currents that have curled lightly within the walls of this place for nearly a century.

In those pews, about 35 chattering folks, teenagers to retirees, slide back and forth along the benches, managing multiple conversations, catching up on the news (no one here would be comfortable with the word "gossip") and mouthing happy "hellos" to folks too far away for a church-appropriate exclamation.

It's cloudy out, but enough light filters through the tall windows to illuminate the interior of this Millsboro church.

A visitor tries to blend into the back wall of the small sanctuary, but he's been to enough of these gatherings to know that is a fool's errand. The service begins and not two minutes in, the Rev. Karen Mumford — a retired mail carrier who has for eight years been the pastor here — raises her eyes in his direction.

"We are so glad to have a visitor here this morning!" she fairly chirps. "Would you mind telling us a little about yourself?"

I've been busted. All heads turn toward me smiling faintly as I rise. I introduce myself and say simply that I'm very happy to be worshiping with everyone here today. Welcoming nods accompany me as I sink back into my place.

I *am* happy to be here. But I have an ulterior motive. For a moment I feel a little like one of Joshua's Old Testament spies, sent to scout our the Promised Land.

But I've blown my cover. Some spy I am.

For a while there, thought I was going in circles.

New to lower Delaware and exploring the countryside by car, I kept driving past the same old church. It was a modest, whitewashed wood affair with a steep, shingled roof and tall, narrow windows on each of its long sides. Spilling out next door was an aged cemetery with its low-lying skyline of headstones and monuments.

It didn't take long, of course, to realize I was stumbling not upon the same church, but instead a perplexing number of them; variations on a theme with architectural differences, subtle and not. They stand in farm fields and on main streets; at crossroads and down country lanes. Some have steeples, some hide their original clapboard under layers of brick, like vintage petticoats kept in storage.

The Netherlands has its groaning windmills; Kansas has its silver grain elevators ... and coastal Delaware has its white chapels.

Most days these old churches stand dark and empty — and indeed there are some that seem utterly abandoned, their dirty windows punctured by rocks, wiregrass threatening to overtake their crumbling sidewalks.

But on any given Sunday morning, many Sunday evenings and even the occasional Wednesday night, the flicker of candles wobbles through the windowpanes of most. As the sound of muffled hymnody filters through the walls, all is pretty much as it has been for, in some cases, nearly two centuries.

Empty or teeming with life, coastal Delaware's old churches bear witness to an otherwise vanishing history. The roads that pass them may be widened and the surrounding farmlands may sprout houses the way they once grew soybeans, but the old churches stand.

Read the historical sign outside any one of the white churches of southern Delaware and you'll most likely find the word "Methodist." More than a few of the buildings have shifted their affiliations over the decades — and some have even changed locations. But Methodism remains a recurring theme.

There's certainly a family resemblance among the old wooden churches, and that has a lot to do with a big brick building up the road a piece. Lots of us heading along Route 1 zip past Barratt's Chapel, north of Milford, without giving it much thought, but for America's 12 million Methodists, Milford is a pretty big deal. It's where two British emissaries sent by Methodism's co-founder John Wesley — Francis Asbury and Thomas Coke — met in 1784 to make plans for the establishment of the Methodist church in America.

"There's the star on the floor," says Barratt's Chapel's historian, Phil Lawton, pointing to a brass plaque embedded at the foot of the pulpit. "We can't really say that's the *exact* spot where the two first met, but anyway that's where the star is." It's a cloudy day, and darkness hides the far corners of the chapel's large interior. Built in 1780, as the cannons were still booming amid the American Revolution, it's the oldest Methodist-built house of worship in the country.

"Really, it's just a barn structurally," says Lawton, leading me up a narrow stairway to the deep balcony — one of two staircases, since men and women once sat separately. "But it's big. Even though people are larger today, we can still get over 500 in here."

The Conleys of Conley's Chapel

Big as it was, that didn't make Barratt's Chapel any easier to get to if you lived on a remote farm. At the time the region was divided into "hundreds," areas that had roughly 100 people (or families — the original rationale for the term is unclear) living in them. The Methodists established a fellowship in each of those hundreds — in homes and taverns at first. Then like pale, pointy mushrooms, small churches started to spring up: the little white churches of southern Delaware.

There's a "family portrait" of those churches hanging in the Barratt's Chapel museum: a wall covered with dozens of vintage ornamental plates, each bearing the image of one small church. Some are spired; some have windows that rise to neo-Gothic points. But they all seem subtly similar, and with good reason.

"If you wanted to build a church in the 19th century, you could buy plans for buildings from the Methodist church," explains Lawton. "You told them whether you wanted wood, brick or stone, and how many people you wanted to seat, and they'd send you plans that you could give to a local carpenter or builder."

Which goes a long way to explaining the striking similarities among the little white structures.

The Lock To Conley Chapel's Choir Loft

One of the best-preserved stands at a corner along Robinsonville Road in Angola by the Bay, where Conley's Chapel has been a center of worship for nearly two centuries. The congregation moved to a new, modern sanctuary a few miles away in 2011, but the old chapel is still home to evening services the second Sunday of each month.

Judy Evans is waiting for me as I push through the front door and into a small vestibule — a feature not all of the little white churches have. Afternoon sun is pouring through the clear glass windows. Outside, the temperature on this late-summer day is pushing 90; in here it's remarkably cool.

"Well, it can get pretty hot," says Evans. "The past couple of months we haven't had the Sunday evening service, because the A/C was out."

Conley's original 1838 chapel was rebuilt in 1876, but Evans pointed out a feature that was most likely a part of the original design: a narrow balcony.

"That's where the slaves sat," she says. "They worshiped here with everyone else." Left hanging in the still chapel air is the essential question: As the voices of enslaved workers wafted above them, singing the same words of the same hymns, just what were the God-fearing people of Conley's thinking?

At the height of American slavery, the Methodist church was outspoken in its opposition to it — yet in Conley's vestibule I can't help but notice that the door to the balcony stairway locks from the outside.

Echoes of slavery sound within many of coastal Delaware's old churches. The present home of Ocean View Presbyterian Church was built in 1907 — although the fellowship traces its history to the late 1600s. In the churchyard stands a memorial to the many slaves who worshiped there, and who are buried in unmarked graves. Another remembers the crew of the *Red Wing*, buried here after their fishing boat sank off the coast in 1891.

"No other church around here would bury them because they didn't know if they were Christian or not," says longtime member Betsy Henifin. "As if that makes any difference!" She seems genuinely tiffed.

Henifin is also part of the church's sewing circle, which has been meeting monthly since 1879.

"We don't actually sew," she confesses, but then the group has always had larger missions in mind. The women of Ocean View Presbyterian were the ones who organized all those burials of the unwanted a century ago. Now they perpetuate the congregation's tradition of inclusiveness through community outreach.

The Presbyterians and Anglicans were actually in southern Delaware before the Methodists, and a few of those centuries-old congregations are splendidly housed in such venerable structures as Lewes Presbyterian Church (founded in 1692; built in 1832) and St. Peter's Episcopal Church in downtown Lewes (founded 1681, built in 1858).

The granddaddy of them all, the Episcopal St. George's Chapel, has stood at its spot along Beaver Dam Road in

Harbeson since 1794, its sturdy bricks having been fired on the site. (It is said that, in the nearby woods, you can still find piles of over-done bricks that had to be discarded.)

St. George's congregation will celebrate its 300th anniversary next year, so of course I must drop in on Amie Sloan, 99, the church's oldest member. She's been attending since 1944.

Sitting on the screened porch of her farmhouse near the bank of Herring Creek, under the watchful eyes of a collection of clay masks she's sculpted over the years, Sloan laughs heartily when I point out she's been alive for one-third of St. George's long history.

"I guess that's true!" she beams. "St. George's is old, and I'm *pretty* old!

"I do remember the oldest person there at the time I started there. She was an old lady who sang off-key!" Sloan laughs again, then turns thoughtful.

"It's such a nice, quiet place. You do think about all the people who were in there before you."

Then she sits, listening to a full-throated choir of cicadas.

Catholics were not legally allowed to vote in Delaware until after the American Revolution — and they weren't terribly welcome even after that — so for centuries Presbyterians, Episcopalians, and Methodists blanketed southern Delaware in Protestant principles. But for sheer influence, with their white church infrastructure in place, nobody could match the Methodists.

As Ocean View Presbyterian Pastor Terence Dougherty cheerily told me, "It's hard to throw a rock in southern Delaware and not hit a Methodist Church."

That social and spiritual homogeny held sway for the better part of a century — until the little white churches slowly evolved into outposts of diversity.

It began, most likely, in 1881, when Harmony Methodist Church, a congregation that still thrives near Millsboro, hired an African-American pastor. That was quite a gesture in an area which had, until just a few years earlier, identified itself strongly with the once-slaveholding South.

But there was one problem: A large portion of the congregation included members of another abused minority, the Nanticoke Indians. Desiring to put their unique stamp on a church of their own, the Indians withdrew from Harmony and established Indian Mission Methodist Church at the corner of Hollyville and Harbeson roads (the name of the latter changes to Indian Mission Road once it crosses Hollyville). If there was ever any residual bitterness between the two congregations, it seems to have evaporated over the past century and a half. And to this day, although attendees include folks of both European and African descent, Indian Mission retains its proud Native American identity.

Indian Mission's Hybrid Banner

The white walls of the sanctuary are punctuated by elements that blend the congregation's Native American and Christian traditions. To the right of the small apse hangs a replica of a feathered headdress. Hanging over the piano is a banner showing the United Methodist Church's emblem — a red flame and a cross — from which five ribbons of bold color radiate: traditional Native American symbols for east (red), west (black), south (yellow), north (white) and the earth (green).

It's midweek, and I'm sitting in the now-quiet sanctuary with longtime member Michele Wright — whose great-grandparents were part of that long-ago split from Harmony Church. I mention the previous week's Pentecost service — the one with the balloons — and I observe that while most Christians are very comfortable discussing the Father and the Son of the Holy Trinity, they are often left grasping to explain the concept of the Holy Spirit.

I suggest that Christians of Native American descent, with their traditional world of spirits and unseen forces, might more easily identify with an ethereal Holy Spirit.

She smiles and nods.

"I think so, because of the spirituality of Native People," she says, noting that, given the elders' teachings and an upbringing steeped in Native American tradition, tribal members are "pretty spiritual to begin with."

Immersed from birth in Indian Mission's unique blending of cultures, Wright can't imagine belonging to a church body anywhere else.

"I was christened here. I was married here. And my spot is out there, under a tree."

"Out there" is the church graveyard, which borders the building on two sides. For those of us so inclined, headstones always make for fascinating reading — but even more so at Indian Mission Church, where the markers often bear both the deceased's Christian and tribal names. So the late Ferdinand Clark is also identified as Chief Sea Gull. And Ingrid Sammons is Smiling Believer.

Wright tells me her tribal name is Hands That Talk, because she speaks sign language. Her husband, a carpenter, is Beaver Spirit.

"You present an elder with some tobacco in their left hand, and ask them to give you a name," she says of the process. "Then that person has to take the time to pray about it."

She chuckles. "You see why spirituality comes so easily to us?"

Blue, aromatic smoke is rising from behind the Rising Sun Masonic Lodge #4 in Milton. It Saturday, it's the summer, and that means the lodge is running its famous (locally, at least) chicken barbecue.

I park on the gravel out front, climb from my car and step back to get a look at the building. It has the unmistakable profile of a 19th century Delaware church, but there are just small, squat windows on the sides. Out back, a fire escape leads to a door on the windowless second story.

The lodge is actually one of coastal Delaware's oldest surviving church buildings, built by Presbyterians in the 1830s. It became a public school in 1872, and in 1892 was bought by the Methodists. (You knew they'd turn up at some point, right?) In 1939 Milton's African-American Masonic Lodge — which had been meeting in various spots around town since 1853 — bought the place.

"I've got the deed somewhere," says Jack Clark. He's the lodge historian, but on this day he's just one of the guys sitting out by the barbecue smoker, shooting the breeze with a couple of pals and resting one hand on his Dalmatian, Pepper.

Right now the lodge has more than 40 active members, down a bit in recent years but still a respectable membership roll by 21st century standards. Well into his 80s, Clark isn't even close to being the lodge's elder statesman — that would be a 102-year-old fellow named Albert who lives down near Salisbury, Md., but still drives to meetings in one of his two cars. Still, Clark's a fourth-generation member, and he tells stories of his grandfather riding to meetings via horse and buggy. His great-grandfather was an illiterate laborer, yet he managed to memorize the rituals required for Masonic membership.

On the first floor inside, they're serving up chicken. I sit there enjoying my lunch — casting a longing eye on the narrow, winding staircase that leads to the dark upper level, the mysterious chamber where lodge rituals and meetings are held. That's how I imagine it, anyway.

"I can take you up there," Clark offers, and I'm ready to go, right now.

But not so fast: "I'll talk with the Worshipful Master and get his OK," he adds, and I sink back into my chair.

I never got that tour. On some level I'm disappointed — but there's a part of me that prefers to imagine some mystical upstairs realm where 102-year-old Masons eat delicious barbecued chicken and commune with the spirits of ancient stonecutters.

In the locked History Room at the Lewes Public Library sits a slim, self-published volume called "Old Country Churches of Sussex County" (don't even *ask* to take it home). The authors included a detailed map locating virtually every historic church in the area, but for the life of me I can't find Landmark Baptist Tabernacle in there.

It makes no sense. Landmark is clearly an old church building, and the place sits prominently along Route 16 in Milton. But it seems to appear in no historic records of old local churches. How could they have missed it?

Easily.

"I had it moved here in 1967," explains Pastor Leslie Freeman, 89, who's headed the congregation ever since he trundled the building on skids from the town of Sycamore, nearly 20 miles southwest of here.

Nattily dressed in a black suit, black shirt, and white tie, Freeman sits with me in the front pew. The Sunday evening service has just ended, and the last of a long line of deferential admirers has wandered off for coffee in the church hall.

"I was looking for a church building to put on this lot, and one day I got a call from a fellow who said, 'I think I've got a church for you!'

"It's a good, solid church," Freeman adds. And it must be: The former Broad Creek Baptist Church was built in 1800, remodeled in 1856 — and the stressful move from Sycamore managed only to crack the old plaster ceiling. The pastor himself replaced it with pinewood. He looks up, still admiring his handiwork.

Landmark is a predominantly black church, but I mention to him I couldn't help noticing more diversity at this service than I've seen elsewhere in the area.

Freeman straightens himself up and beams, as if I've just complimented his fine haircut.

"It's the way it should be," he says.

As a young black minister, Freeman watched in despair as the churches of southern Delaware continued on the racially segregated path they had followed for centuries.

"I remember attending a tent meeting in Selbyville," he says. "I was like a fly in a pan of milk!"

He encouraged local white people to attend his church, leading to some curious questions from his congregation.

"They asked me, 'Preacher, is this a black church or a white church?'" he recalls. "I told them, 'Neither — it's a Christian church.' I'd had enough of that."

We've been sitting there for the better part of an hour, chatting about old-time tent meetings and Freeman's early days as a mechanic — he still owns Freeman's Auto Salvage in Lincoln — when his wife steps in from the church hall to fetch him.

Her name is Marva. They call her "Marvelous." We say good night, and Marva gently takes her husband's arm. The man who built this church with soul, sweat and a heart for people of all races disappears through the doorway to the church hall.

I step out into the night, to the sound of traffic rumbling along Route 16. As I wend my way through the back roads home, I pass no fewer than four little white churches; witnesses to the past, heralds of the future.

Joshua's spies came back reporting they'd seen giants in the Promised Land.

So have I.

Jim and Lorna Landis Feel No Need To Branch Out

THE CHRISTMAS TREE FARMERS

Christmas comes every day for Jim and Lorna Landis — and it's exhausting.

For 52 weeks a year, the couple and their staff sweat through a never-ending cycle of planting, digging, irrigating, and shearing thousands upon thousands of Christmas trees. And there's no escaping it at the end of the day: The windows of the couple's rambling house look right out on their 21-acre spread.

"Yep," says Jim, scanning the never-ending evergreen landscape. "It's a lot of trees."

Christmas trees have been a growing concern for the Landises ever since they planted their first firs at Harbeson's Landis Tree Farm in 1991 — and even longer for Lorna, whose grandfather and father both cut and sold trees. Jim, who's retired from the insurance business (Lorna is a former banker) takes care of the day-to-day business of tree farming.

Jim invites me for a ride on a golf cart. As we bounce through the grassy, tree-studded field, I'm amazed by just how many different kinds of Christmas trees there are.

"We've got about 11,000 trees right now," he says. "So I guess there's something for everybody.

"A few years ago we sold a tree that was 20-23 feet tall. For a guy's living room!"

I wonder aloud if anyone ever came around looking for a scraggly Charlie Brown tree.

"Oh, yeah!" he says. "We've had people come in here looking just for a little tree, one that we've probably just planted, that you wouldn't think could hold a single ornament."

As the regiment of evergreens passes in review, I observe that they don't really look like Christmas trees. They're all — how shall I put this gently — kind of bedraggled.

"You're right!" Landis says, clearly happy that I've raised the subject.

"People are surprised to learn that Christmas trees don't naturally have that nice, conical shape. They have to be sheared. My wife and I shear the pines and my son comes in and shears the fir trees. He's got a pair of stilts he wears to get up to the high spots.

"The thing about growing Christmas trees is, you've got to be doing something every month of the year."

It seems to me as back-to-basics as a business can get — even more rudimentary than traditional farming. You dig a hole, you plant a tree, you wait for it to grow, you cut it down.

But Landis surprises me again by explaining that there's such a thing as Christmas tree technology, along with actual professional journals.

"I've read some things recently about a hybrid between a balsam fir and a Frasier fir," he says, assuming a professorial tone.

"I don't think they've produced a whole lot of seeds, so they can't put them on the market yet. That should be a good mix, because needle retention will still be very good, and you will be able to grow them in a warmer area.

"In any case, it would be at least eight years before you could buy one — that's how long it takes before a tree is big enough to sell."

I ask Landis to show me his most exotic Christmas tree. He makes a sharp turn and drives me out to the back of the property. There, he proudly points to a row of stubby little tree-like bushes not more than two feet high.

"They're Korean firs," he says, almost reverently. "Very slow-growing. The oldest ones have been out here for about five years and you can see how short they are.

"I'm just waiting on them to see what happens. It's one of my experiments. My son doesn't like them. He says we've got to put things in the ground that grow fast!"

Ah, the impatience of youth. Just like Christmas morning.

The Author Sun Spotting (Photo by Carolyn Newcott)

THE TELESCOPE IN THE CEMETERY

It is 2 p.m. on June 3 and people are looking at me. Or, rather, they are looking at my reflecting telescope, set on its tripod just beyond the low brick wall of Bethel Methodist Cemetery along Savannah Road in Lewes.

No one stops to ask me what I'm doing with this primarily nocturnal instrument, surrounded by headstones and pointed directly at the sun. I wish someone would, because it's a fascinating story.

At least I think so.

The fact is, I'm engaged in a reenactment of sorts: At this specific location, at this precise second, on this exact date 251 years ago, a team of astronomers dispatched to Lewes by none other than Benjamin Franklin himself observed the small black disk of the planet Venus traversing the face of the sun.

In so doing — in concert with astronomers taking similar measurements at that moment from locales across the globe — they helped define the size of the solar system to a level of precision that rivals the most exacting modern calculations.

And, dear reader, if that does not get your juices flowing, I'd suggest you flip right now to the restaurant guide in the back of this issue. Because we're about to wander, starry-eyed, into the realm of monumental historical nerdishness — and the personal passion of a modern Rehoboth Beach resident whose obsession with stars, time and historical instruments enabled me to stand confidently on the spot where 18th century scientific history was made.

It was on May 26, 1769, that three gentlemen arrived in Lewes by boat from Philadelphia. Owen Biddle was a prominent Philadelphia clock maker; Joel Bailey was an experienced surveyor who had helped define the Mason-Dixon Line; Richard Thomas — no known relation to the actor who played John Boy on "The Waltons" — was a prominent Philadelphia surveyor. We can only imagine how strange they looked unloading their exotic cargo, including three reflecting telescopes, a surveyor's theodolite, and a full-sized pendulum clock.

It was odd enough when the trio immediately rented an empty house on Fourth Street. But when they approached two local schoolboys for a mysterious task, the weirdness of these visitors must have seemed positively flummoxing.

Most likely, it helped that they had been dispatched here by the great Ben Franklin, who even then was a living legend. As a leading light of the Philadelphia Philosophical Society, Franklin had aligned himself with London's Royal Astronomical Society (remember, the Revolutionary War was not to erupt for another six years) in its quest to determine the vast distances of outer space.

In 1769, every astronomer worth his salt knew the planet Venus was scheduled to pass before the sun around 2 p.m. Colonial time on June 3 — and that the phenomenon would not occur again until

1874. Through separate observations of the event from enough spots across the face of the Earth, scientists would be able to accurately measure not only the distance to the sun, but by extension the size of the entire known solar system.

Franklin enthusiastically joined the project. Three North American locations, widely separated to mitigate the chance of weather problems, were chosen for observations: Philadelphia's Statehouse Square (now known as Independence Square); the Pennsylvania farm of David Rittenhouse, America's leading astronomer; and Lewes.

A backwater town at the mouth of Delaware Bay may seem like a strange choice for participation in a global scientific study, but Franklin had a double mission in mind. In order to precisely measure the transit of Venus, the Lewes team would first need to conduct an extensive survey to determine their exact latitude and longitude — information that could also be used to pinpoint the location of the brand-new Cape Henlopen lighthouse, which had been lit for the first time earlier that year.

The guys had just eight days to prepare. A land survey requires a known starting point, and the only relatively handy one was the recently surveyed Transpeninsular Line in Fenwick — the very same one Mason and Dixon used to determine the starting point of their famous line separating Maryland and Pennsylvania. Working feverishly with a small crew of local workers, in less than four days Bailey and Thomas surveyed a distance of some 20 miles across farms, forests, and ponds from Fenwick to Lewes, following Colonial-era roads and trails whenever possible.

Combining these ground measurements with several nights of astronomical observations (including the positions of Jupiter's moons), Bailey set the precise location of the rented house in Lewes. Using his coordinates, that would put the house roughly at the intersection of Pilottown Road and Shipcarpenter Street, right near the Lewes Historical Society campus.

So, why am I standing with my telescope in a cemetery nearly a half-mile from there? Allow me to introduce you to Jim Morrison, a now-deceased Oklahoma-born engineer who worked briefly for the U.S. space program in California before settling in for a long career at IBM. He retired to the Rehoboth area and became fascinated with Lewes' connection to the 1769 transit of Venus.

"I'm not sure when his fascination with astronomical measurements started," says his son, Chris Morrison, a photographer for a Kansas City, Missouri., TV station. "But sometime when I was a kid he became fascinated with sundials: how they worked, why they worked, the angles involved, all of that."

Then came an infinitely more exotic pursuit: astrolabes, the baroque devices sailors used for centuries to steer by the stars.

"He actually found a way to simulate a physical astrolabe on a computer," says Morrison.

Museums often publish lushly illustrated books of astrolabes from their collections, treating them more like works of art than scientific instruments. In 2007, Jim Morrison tried to fill that gap with a painstakingly researched book on all things astrolabe. Titled "The Astrolabe," it's out of print now, but if you go on Amazon you can pick up a paperback copy for $499, shipping included.

Naturally, as a resident of the Lewes-Rehoboth Beach area, an astronomical enthusiast like Morrison could not ignore the 1769 transit of Venus. Reading Biddle's account, he couldn't help but think there was something wrong about the accepted location of the observatory. For one thing, Biddle clearly stated that he had rented a house on South Street (now Savannah Road) about .02 miles southwest of Fourth Street. That would put it a lot closer to today's Beebe Healthcare than the Lewes Historical Society.

It was, then, in the spirit of Ben Franklin's alliance with London's Royal Astronomical Society that Morrison teamed up with Geoff Thurston, a member of the British Astronomical Society. Together they drafted a scholarly paper recalculating every measurement Biddle and his team made. They considered how Biddle presumed a spherical shape of the Earth when it is now known to be more of an ellipsoid. They found occasional cases of transposed numbers in Biddle's calculations.

Superimposing the reported route of Bailey and Thomas on a Google Maps grid, they found a consistent degree of shift from known roads.

In the end, Morrison and Thurston painted a digital bull's-eye on this spot where I'm standing in the Bethel Methodist Cemetery: close to the road, right where the front yard of a 17th century house would have been, the main street ensuring there would be few trees to block the view of the early afternoon sky.

Aside from some clouds, the sky I now stand under matches perfectly the one Biddle, Bailey, and Thomas beheld, the sun nearly straight above my head. My telescope is aimed sunward, just as theirs were — but of course I'm not going to look into that eyepiece. I don't want to incinerate my retina. Biddle and Bailey placed heavily smoked glass in front of their telescopes, but even then it was dangerous to gaze at the sun too long. So they glanced through the glass periodically, waiting for the moment, hoping they'd be looking just when the dark circle of Venus began to appear.

Biddle did not know the exact time when Venus would pierce the sun's horizon — around 2 p.m. was the best anyone could figure. But he was not depending on a pocket watch to alert him. In order to establish the precise local time, the pendulum clock he'd floated in from Philadelphia had been set at the exact moment the sun was at its zenith.

It is 2 p.m. I stand back from my telescope. Through the eyepiece I can see that intense, focused solar light. A few blocks from here, in the 355-year-old Ryves Holt House on Second Avenue, I know the shadows on the floor match perfectly those that were cast the day Biddle and Bailey looked hopefully into their eyepieces.

Their echoes sound around me.

The moment arrives. Biddle momentarily averts his view through the telescope. Bailey lets out a shout. Biddle peers again

— and lets out a gasp. There it is: A tiny, nibble-size crescent has already been bitten out of the sun.

"Now!" he yells.

Immediately, those two schoolboys Biddle hired begin chanting out the seconds — taking turns minute by minute — following the beats of the swinging clock pendulum. For the scientists looking through their telescopes, it's an 18th century version of a digital countdown clock superimposed on the image of the sun. The scientists look away from their eyepieces only long enough to write down the times Venus initially touches the sun's disk (first contact) and when it is fully inside it (second contact).

Biddle is cursing himself for having missed first contact, but Bailey got a good look and logs Venus' first appearance 2:11:53 p.m. Importantly, both men get the same time for second contact: 2:29.53. Eighteen minutes in all, to the second.

Of 171 field observations made that day across the hemisphere, the Lewes data was considered to be among the most meticulously collected. Mathematicians in London pored over the numbers and calculated that the distance from Earth to the sun — a value known as an astronomical unit — was about 95.37 million miles.

Our best number today: Some 93 million. That's about a 2 percent error. Not bad for a bunch of guys rolling telescopes around in wooden wagons.

There is a photo of Rehoboth's Jim Morrison, bent over a reflecting telescope in a spot that looks to be Cape Henlopen State Park. He is observing a transit of Venus — only the fourth since Bailey, Biddle and Thomas lugged their paraphernalia from Philadelphia to Lewes. His excitement seems to reach out through the camera. This is the sort of thing he lives for.

I look at the photo and I'm glad Jim Morrison lived long enough to have that moment. He died on April 8, 2012, which in one of those cosmic coincidences happens to be the 280th anniversary of the birth of David Rittenhouse — the Philadelphia astronomer Ben Franklin had handpicked to head the transit of Venus project.

After planning for a year and dispatching Biddle's team to Lewes, on June 3, 1769, Rittenhouse finally sat down to observe the event he'd anticipated for so long.

But Rittenhouse didn't see first contact.

He had fainted.

Full Moon Over Fiddler's Hill

THE GHOST OF FIDDLER'S HILL

Sealed in our air-conditioned SUVs, accelerating into country turns like racers at Le Mans, we seldom slow ourselves, roll down the windows, and soak in the intimate sights and whispering sounds that surround us.

And maybe that's why we've never heard the plaintive strains of the Ghost of Fiddler's Hill.

You have almost certainly encountered Fiddler's Hill. Heading south on Robinsonville Road, about six miles from Lewes, the route makes a sudden right-hand turn, then an abrupt left, and then passes through a wooded area stretching a few hundred yards. As you ascend slightly, you are climbing what is locally known as Fiddler's Hill.

I'm a sucker for ghost stories, and Fiddler's Hill has a pretty good one. Even the town of Robinsonville is a ghost: According to the U.S. Geological Survey, the long-gone settlement of Robinsonville sat, you guessed it, right atop Fiddler's Hill.

But that's not the half of it: This little patch of ground is steeped in folklore and history — both vividly recent and veiled in the misty past. There's a reason Robinsonville Road makes those strange turns just north of Fiddler's Hill: This is where the road crosses the upper reaches of Love Creek. In Colonial times, bridges were always built at a right angle to the streams below in order to make the spans as short as possible. As a result, roads — which might approach a brook from any direction — often had to make sharp turns on either side of a bridge.

In the late 1600s, just upstream from the site of this particular bridge, a man named Jonathan Bailey built a dam and erected a mill. The 300-foot earthen dam — which created what is today known as Goslee Mill Pond — was built from soil excavated just to the south and transported by men driving ox carts.

All that digging left behind a crater that to this day is referred to as "The Dirt Hole." It's a secluded, wooded depression that for decades was occupied seasonally by itinerant tradespeople. They arrived in wagons each fall and stayed for two or three weeks. "A jolly and happy band of people, they dressed in colorful clothing and danced at night by firelight," reported the late Rhea Warrington, a longtime area resident whose family owned the mill, in a paper she wrote in 1978. "They made their living by telling fortunes and trading. ... The area became known as Gypsies Landing."

Phil Jackson, now in his mid-70s, remembers them from his childhood. "They were there in their wagons," he tells me. "Nice people. They came every year."

A member of the Nanticoke Indian tribe, Jackson was educated barely a quarter-mile from here — again, up on Fiddler's Hill — in a one-room segregated schoolhouse that was until 1965 strictly for Native American and African American children. Today the 100-year-old Rabbit's Ferry School serves as a community center — and also as a daily reminder of Sussex County's dark days of persistent racial segregation.

"Rabbit's Ferry?" you're asking. "There was a ferry across Love Creek?"

Not exactly. The short version, according to everyone I asked: During a community gathering on the school grounds many years ago, a rabbit came dashing right across a picnic blanket. Someone exclaimed, "That rabbit just ferried across our blanket!" and the name was born (A lame explanation, I know, but we're stuck with it).

The old mill was long gone when Jackson built his home on the south side of Goslee Mill Pond in the early 1980s, but Robinsonville Road was still a gravel byway with a rickety wooden bridge spanning Love Creek. Sitting in a shady gazebo Jackson has placed just above the rebuilt dam, I watch clouds reflected on the pond's still surface, listening to the music of water rushing through the spillway. Even though some development has arisen on the far side of the pond, the shore is still guarded, at least for now, by an unbroken palisade of tall trees.

"If you ever feel bad about anything," Jackson says, "you just sit by that pond, listening to that water coming over the dam, and you'll feel good again."

On the far side of the dam is the home of Tom Downs, a retired education consultant who built his place around the same time Jackson moved in. "Back then, this pond was completely choked with grass," Downs says, leading me behind his wooden house to the water's edge. "Looking at it, you'd swear you could just walk across."

Along with Jackson, Downs set to work dragging the grass from the pond. It took weeks, but in the end they'd revealed one of the loveliest bodies of water in all of Delaware.

I ask both men if they're familiar with the story of the Ghost of Fiddler's Hill. "Where'd you hear that story?" Jackson says with a laugh, surprised. "I've always known that story, but I didn't think other people did."

As we sit in his living room, Downs shows me a framed work of calligraphy that tells the tale. It's a disappointingly brief account of two men courting the same woman, a sudden death, and a tortured spirit whose anguished song can still be heard. No dates, no names. A skeleton of a story.

I thank Downs, carefully back my car onto busy Robinsonville Road — and as I head up Fiddler's Hill, my writer's mind feverishly starts to embellish the bare-bones yarn. By the time I get home I've stitched together all the threads, historic and mythic, that I've gathered about this remarkably rich square in the quilt of coastal Delaware.

So, gather ye round, children, whilst I relate the unexpurgated tale of the Ghost of Fiddler's Hill.

Centuries ago in coastal Delaware, every road was rutted by wagon wheels, neighbors lived miles apart, and if you planned to drive from Lewes to Millsboro, well, you'd best have found a place to spend the night.

In the remote village of Robinsonville there lived a most comely young woman named Effie Robinson. As her last name implied, she was the only child of an influential local businessman and landowner. So beautiful was Effie Robinson — and so influential was her father — that young men from all over the county of Sussex made the jostling journey along Robinsonville Road to seek her hand. She was kind and patient with all of them, but only two caught her fancy: A dashing, freckle-faced shipbuilder's son from Lewes ... and a poor but charming fiddle-playing boy from Gypsies Landing, near the Love Creek mill.

Finally, Effie told the fiddler and the shipbuilder's son that she would choose between them come the full moon. She asked them both to visit her that evening, at which time she would reveal her decision.

The night arrived. The poor fiddler boy despaired of being Effie's favored one — he knew there was no way her domineering father would ever approve of his fair-skinned daughter marrying a swarthy wanderer, not when there was a blond-haired shipbuilder's son in the picture. So he devised a plan: He would climb with his fiddle into a tree along the rising road to Robinsonville and, when his rival came into view in his horse-drawn wagon, he would burst into a screeching tune that sounded like music from the very gates of hell. He hoped that the shipbuilder's son, convinced he was being assailed by demons, would turn his cart around and rush back to Lewes, never to be seen again.

Much to his delight (and surprise), the scheme worked! The sound of the boy's fiddle cut through the moonlit night like the howl of a banshee. Screaming and swearing, Effie's would-be beau yanked on the reins of his rearing horse, whipped the wagon around and sent his cart careening back down the hill.

But the plot went horribly wrong: Heading too fast into the sharp left turn before the old wooden bridge, the wagon crashed to one side. The boy was thrown like a rag doll. He plunged into the creek. From his perch on a high tree limb, the Gypsy boy could clearly see his rival was dead. Shock seized the young fiddler. His foot slipped on the dew-covered branch. Arms flailing, barely stifling a scream, he plummeted to the gravel road below, his neck snapping with a sickening crack.

Effie had been up all night fretting about her two suitors when someone knocked on the front door with the tragic news. The fiddler boy had been found in the road. The shipbuilder's son was discovered in Love Creek, grotesquely splayed across the rocks, a family of rabbits ferrying across the stream on his twisted body.

Heartbroken, Effie vowed never to marry. She died a year later of a broken heart. Devastated, her parents moved away from Robinsonville. And to ensure the sad story died for good, they bought up the properties in the village and had the whole place leveled, mill and all.

But the sorrow of tragic love lives forever. Sitting by the gurgling spillway on a quiet evening, you may still hear the rattling of the doomed wagon as it tries to rush across Love Creek. And in the dark of night, as you come upon the rise where the cursed town of Robinsonville once stood, the sound of plaintive fiddle music sometimes floats above the trees. As an old Delaware folk song warns,

> *When the moon is full*
> *And the air is still,*
> *Ye can still hear the Ghost*
> *Of Fiddler's Hill.*

For Fabrice Veron, Every Day Is Tanksgiving

THINK TANK

There is nothing more irresistible to me than a sign that reads, in effect, "Keep Out."

Without fail — you just know it — there is something absolutely fascinating going on beyond that sign. Even better, there's also probably someone hellbent on keeping you from finding out what that something is.

Much of my career has been spent trying to get past "Keep Out" signs, so you can imagine my delight one recent day in Cape Henlopen State Park when I spotted a large gray building, right near the fishing pier, with a startling array of signs bearing some of the most fantastic cautions I've ever read:

"WARNING!!! DO NOT ENTER IF THE SIGN IS FLASHING. EXPERIMENT IN PROGRESS"

"VISIBLE AND/OR INVISIBLE LASER RADIATION — AVOID EYE OR SKIN EXPOSURE TO DIRECT OR SCATTERED RADIATION"

So many exclamation marks! This I had to see.

A far more prosaic sign stands a few feet from the thrillingly ominous ones, identifying the building as something called the Air-Sea Interaction Lab, a facility belonging to the University of Delaware's College of Earth, Ocean and Environment.

Not the sort of establishment you'd expect to be dabbling in death-ray lasers that will simultaneously blind you and cause your skin to slough, I thought. So I placed a call and set up a visit with the lab's director, who happens to have the coolest name of anyone I've met since moving to Delaware: Fabrice Veron.

"I was born in France," says Veron, explaining his fantastic name (magazine style demands I henceforth refer to him as Veron, which is too bad because Fabrice is just too good to use only once).

As Veron greets me at the facility door, I am slightly disappointed to see that the mad scientist I'd been hoping for is actually a soft-spoken, bearded fellow with an easy smile and quick laugh.

Veron is one of the world's foremost experts on ocean waves. Raised near the sea, he loves scuba diving. In school he developed an early interest in mechanical engineering and then, as a musician, in acoustics.

"My 'aha' moment came when I was in grad school — I realized acoustic waves are a lot like ocean waves," Veron says. "This was a way to combine all my interests."

It's just a few steps from the door to the building's centerpiece, a 138-foot-long wind-wave channel: basically a mega fish tank (*sans* fish) mounted about 15 feet above the concrete floor. The tank itself is about four feet deep and three feet wide with rectangular panels of glass that extend for its entire length. The contraption resembles a subway car, or a monorail — only if you were to open a door in the side of this train some 8,000 gallons of water would come pouring out.

The tank was built 40 years ago, dedicated on June 20, 1979. This building, a former Fort Miles munitions depot, was not only large enough to contain the tank, it also had a solid concrete floor strong enough to support the massive weight of the machine plus all the water inside.

As the lab's name suggests, Veron and his colleagues use the tank to study the interaction of the ocean surface with the air above it. They create waves in the tank two ways: with wind, created by a fan at one end, or with a mechanical wave maker that physically pushes the water into action.

The entire tank also tilts at one end to create currents that will interact with the waves, just as they do in the ocean.

In fact, Veron says with some pride, "this is the only tilting wind-wave channel in the world. People come from all over the planet to work on it."

The wave-making mechanism is being serviced on this day, so Veron turns on the wind fan. At first a small ripple action appears on the water surface; soon actual waves, about a quarter-inch high, develop.

Then Veron starts saying things that blow my mind.

"We really don't know how waves are formed," he says, and I think he's kidding.

But seriously: "What you just witnessed here — waves forming from blowing wind — we don't really understand it.

"I tell my students if they were to aim a hair dryer into a full bathtub — and I also say they shouldn't do that — but if they did, those ripples would start to form from the blowing air. And we don't really know why that happens. The pressure variations in the air are not enough to make waves."

What else don't we know?

"Hurricanes are very mysterious," he says, and I can sense his excitement rising. "In some ways, they're relatively simple. We know there are two dynamics working on a hurricane: The hurricane gets its energy by removing heat from the ocean, and the ocean removes energy from the hurricane by causing friction at the surface.

"But when we did the math, figuring how much energy a hurricane could pull from the ocean's surface and how much energy the water surface pulled from the hurricane, we came to a surprising conclusion: There should be no such thing as a hurricane! Hurricanes don't exist! There's not enough energy being transferred."

Now, in the Cape Henlopen wave tank, Veron and his fellow wizards are trying to solve that puzzle by studying spray — the water droplets tossed into the air by violent wave action — to see if that's where the missing energy is coming from.

"Water droplets are very efficient in transferring energy," he says. "It's why you're chilly after taking a shower.

"We're literally trying to measure how many droplets get ejected by a breaking wave."

Plus, he adds, since the winds of a hurricane only encounter friction at the tops of waves — rather than across the entire surface of the sea — it's possible the effect of friction removing energy from storms has been overestimated in the past. If Veron and company can crack that energy transfer puzzle, scientists may be able to improve predictions of hurricane strength.

But what about the killer laser beams promised by the signs outside? Where is the Frankenstein monster lab equipment I'd been hoping to see?

Veron points to a nondescript array mounted atop the tank. "That's it up there," he says. The powerful lasers are used to create cross-section views of the water in motion and artificial fog floating above it, basically CAT scans of wave and air activity. The windows at the point where the beams enter the water from above are shielded with black shrouds, but water and fog diffuse light, so everybody in the lab has to be extremely careful and don goggles when the lasers are zapping.

Veron has waves to study, so it's time for me to wave goodbye. I knew this would be fascinating, I tell him as he escorts me to the door.

"It *is* fascinating," he smiles. "For a geek like me, anyway."

Well, sign me up for the Geek Squad.

Jayne's Reliable In Dagsboro

GETTING LOST

For the seasoned traveler, there's nothing better than getting lost. If you never get lost, you never discover anything.

Alas, getting lost isn't as easy as it sounds — particularly if you're determined to get lost in the place where you live. There are street signs everywhere. Familiar landmarks keep popping up. And you have to resist the urgent temptation to switch on your GPS, "just to see."

Despite the challenges, I was determined to get lost in coastal Delaware for a whole day; to explore unfamiliar back roads; to meet people who didn't know anybody I knew. And so one recent morning I kissed my wife farewell, hopped into my car, and set out to get utterly disoriented.

Of course, even getting lost requires ground rules. I decided on a specific starting point and a final destination, to reduce the chances of just driving around in circles all day. Point A would be the Fenwick Island Lighthouse, hard up against the

Delaware/Maryland border. Point Z would be Cape Henlopen, site of the Fenwick light's long-lost sister, the beacon that fell from its sand dune pulpit in 1926.

As for my random route, from Fenwick I would improvise a wide westward loop around the area's inland waterways.

Most importantly, I brought up the GPS function on my iPhone and swiped it away. Gone. No familiar voice telling me where to turn. No scrolling dashboard map.

I smiled smugly.

"This is how Daniel Boone must have felt," I thought, sipping hazelnut coffee from my travel mug.

1. I start at the lighthouse

I am standing at the foot of the whitewashed Fenwick Island light, craning to see the black lantern room, eight stories above.

Actually, I'm standing in Maryland. The Delaware state line, inches north of the sidewalk, is defined by a low white monument, placed here on April 16, 1751. The Maryland side of the monument bears the familiar diamond-and-cross design of the Calvert family coat of arms. The Penn family crest on the Delaware side recalls when the state was still part of Pennsylvania. Happily, in 1776 nascent Delawareans simultaneously declared their independence from both King George III and Pennsylvania — lest they someday refer to submarine sandwiches as hoagies and say things like "Yinz go'n to the Steelers game, yah?"

This monument tells me exactly where I am. That will not do.

There's only one route west out of Fenwick Island: Lighthouse Road, also called Route 54. I cross the bridge over The Ditch, a canal that separates Little Assawoman Bay from her sister, Big Assawoman Bay.

I live up near Lewes, where a favorite parlor game is to come up with creative profane names for the developers who'll tear down a forest, evict all the animals and rechristen the place "The Preserve." We tend to think enviously of less-developed Fenwick and its environs, but my neighbors would be shocked at the amount of building going on down here. Everywhere I look, communities are springing up; field after field of "stick-built" homes (a term that makes me imagine Little Pig construction crews). Nevertheless, I've never been along this stretch of road before. I'm not quite lost yet, but I'm at least exploring the unknown.

Standing In Maryland

2. I try to get lost

Not far up the road, even at 35 mph, I am aware of eyes watching me. I glance to the left and stare back at the faces peering from the windows of Sound United Methodist Church.

It's a century-old building in the style of so many country churches around here, but Sound Church has one distinctive feature: an array of gloriously colorful stained-glass windows, each combining the Old World art of colored glass with a decidedly folk-art-inspired design.

Angels cavort, Jesus extends his hands over the faithful. The colors are bold, the figures flat, like subjects of a Grandma Moses painting.

I'm barely five miles out of Fenwick and already my wanderings are rewarding me.

A bit farther along, I hang a random left on Williamsville Road. It's winding and it grows narrower by the half-mile. I pass an abandoned chicken house with three turkey vultures on the roof, waiting for the welcome whiff of a rotting carcass. In an empty field I spot a miniature concrete lighthouse, maybe 15 feet tall, seemingly awaiting someone to build a miniature golf course around it. Today I'll spot dozens of lawn lighthouses, persistent reminders that although I'm surrounded by farmland, the sea is never far away.

The pavement becomes rougher. I'll later learn this is the point where Williamsville Road dips briefly into Maryland — its name changing ironically to Delaware Road — before looping back into the First State. I seem to be pushing deeper and deeper into a bayside wilderness. I couldn't be happier.

Then I make a turn, and my illusions of remote wild lands are shattered. Spreading before me, like a stick-built Oz, stands the sprawling Bayside development, home of the Freeman Stage.

A bit deflated, I drive to the end of the property, where a poolside restaurant overlooks Big Assawoman Bay. Across the water, seemingly close enough to touch, are the towering condos of Ocean City.

I'm not lost at all.

3. I find the Land of Lost RVs

You don't pass up a street called Bearhole Road. So I turn onto it, keeping a hopeful lookout for bears, or the holes that contain them.

A mile or so in I find something almost as good: a lineup of life-size plywood cartoon figures atop a low hill. There's a smiling guy in what may be blue bathing trunks carrying what looks like a hatchet. He's running away from an angry blond woman wielding a roller pin, and she's followed by several other amused characters, including a child pulling a dog.

Behind this odd crew stretches a long red chicken barn — a "chicken house," in local parlance — surrounded by lots of RV campers. And on the roof, in letters large enough to be seen by passing aircraft, are the words: "Lost Lands RV Park — Where Country Meets the Beach."

I pull into the gravel drive and park at the near end of the barn. The structure is enormous, stretching toward a vanishing point like the work of a young artist just getting the hang of depicting perspective.

"It's 500 feet long," says David Simpson, the friendly owner of Lost Lands and the closest thing to a mayor for this collection of 179 motor homes. He's been running the place for 19 years.

"It was an abandoned chicken farm," says Simpson, a bearded, ball-capped native of the area. "No one was looking after it. We had to clear off the hog pens and the tractors and the old cars."

Simpson is especially proud of his renovation of the chicken house, nearly long enough to contain a horizontal Washington Monument. Aside from an international airport terminal or cathedral, you don't often step into a long, unobstructed enclosed space like this. There are picnic tables for its entire length — a place for the RV park residents to dine and, perhaps, create a small sense of community. The interior is decorated with old road signs and other whimsical touches, including an array of mounted bedpans.

Simpson tells me he didn't expect to become an RV park impresario; he stumbled upon this place completely by accident.

"I'm just one of those guys who likes to go out on the back roads and see what's there," he says. "I like to not just see things, but look *through* things, and envision what they could be."

Then he smiles.

"Like you," he says.

Bearhole Road has been good to me, so I continue on it straight to the end. I flip a coin, make a few random turns, and end up on the wonderfully named Gum Road.

That's when I see the horse. I think it's a Clydesdale, but who am I kidding? I know horses like I know quantum physics. Maybe less. But I have to pull over to admire his striking coat and four white "socks." His long blond mane is a torrent of hair spilling over his shoulders, nearly to his knees.

I Am Being Watched

I pull over to take a picture of him grazing. But the moment I raise my camera, he lifts his head to stare at me.

"I don't want a portrait — I want a candid!" I mutter. But he stares me down until I leave.

4. I meet the Redmen

I head west on Gum Road, named for the family of 17th century farmer Roger Gum, whose genetic line nearly 250 years later yielded a Minnesota girl named Frances Gumm — better known to you and me as Judy Garland.

I pass farm houses with cars parked on the grass and solitary houses built on lots that were covered with corn not long ago. Just outside of downtown Selbyville I spot a sign for Cemetery Road.

It probably says a lot about me when I say my idea of a good time is exploring an old cemetery. In Selbyville Redmen's

Cemetery I spot the final resting place of John Townsend Jr., who was governor of Delaware until 1921 (and later a U.S. senator).

The cemetery is named for the Red Men, a fraternal group still in existence but much in decline — and what fraternal group isn't? — that traces its origins back to the Boston Tea Party (in which white Colonists disguised themselves as "red men" to protest British tea taxes). There are Red Men — and Redmen's, as spellings vary — cemeteries like this one across the country.

For some time Selbyville's chief claim to fame was the old Mumford Sheet Metal Works, which in 1950 produced the world's largest frying pan. And Doyle's Restaurant, circa 1930s, is said to be the oldest operating diner in Delaware. These days the town's biggest employer has to be Mountaire Farms. It is lunchtime, and I can easily spot workers from the chicken processing plant, still wearing their gauzy hairnets. One such couple is walking across Church Street. She is clearly trying to stay one step ahead of him; he's trying to keep up without looking like he's actually chasing her.

"You want some of this ice cream cone?" he's yelling, and I can see he's waving a vanilla cone in the air. "You want a bite of this?"

She picks up her pace. "I don't want none of that ice cream cone now!" she shrieks without turning her head. "Not now I don't!"

"Here!" he bellows, desperation rising in his voice. "Take a bite! Take the whole thing! The whole thing!"

She stops and spins in his direction.

"You idiot!" she sobs. "This is *not* about the ice cream cone!"

Even I know that.

5. I traverse the Great Plains

Pepper Road out of Selbyville heads north. Along this stretch of farmland, more than a few families seem to be having yard sales of the most unorganized kind: items from toasters to encyclopedias strewn about on blankets and dropcloths.

It's about 5 miles from Selbyville to Frankford, and unlike the shore communities, which all seem to blend into each other, the gaps between towns make the landscape here feel positively Midwestern.

That Great Plains vibe only grows more vivid as I turn onto

The Grain Elevators Of Frankford

Main Street in Frankford. At one end of the thoroughfare stands the spire of the 167-year-old Frankford United Methodist Church — its silhouette entangled in the towering grain elevators of yet another Mountaire facility. The Cathedrals of the Midwest, they call grain elevators out there, and at this moment I could just as easily be sitting outside Lincoln, Nebraska, as in Slower Lower Delaware.

I leave town, heading northeast on Murray Road, and suddenly I am in horse country. Beyond the low houses on my left I can see oval tracks with red-coated thoroughbreds grazing at their centers.

Seemingly in a flash, I've traveled from America's breadbasket to the bluegrass of Kentucky.

6. I encounter a rocket ship

It's one thing to get lost; it's quite another to shift space/time. One moment I'm trying to find my way through Dagsboro — the next I'm blinded by the afternoon sun glinting off a sleek silver rocket ship. Squinting into the light, I see the craft is sailing across the lawn of a large century-old house.

The rocket is a piece of art, it's for sale, and that goes for everything inside and outside the fanciful jumble that is Jayne's Reliable, where a quick glance around reveals choice offerings including a bronze mermaid, some rusting vintage gas station signs, and an ancient doctor's office scale.

"Yeah, the rocket gets a lot of people in," says Karen Jayne, who came to Dagsboro with her husband, David, to start the business about eight years ago.

"We'd always done other things for a living, but our idea of a good date was always going to a yard sale. We have three grown sons, and we always preached to them, 'Do what you love.' Finally, we decided to follow our own advice."

The Jaynes are purebred collectors — they leave the curating to their customers. So at their emporium you can find that church pew, 8mm film projector, or Coastal Highway street sign you've been looking for. Why you want it, and what you do with it, is nobody's business but yours.

7. I find New England

I'm threading the needle between Dupont Boulevard, also known as Route 113 — as far west as I'm willing to go — and the upper reaches of the Indian River on Iron Branch Road, which becomes State Street. There's no way to be lost here, but as I approach Main Street in downtown Millsboro, I realize I've never crossed it and continued north. So I head that way, staying on State Street — and am almost immediately rewarded with one of the loveliest stretches of road in all of coastal Delaware.

It begins where State Street becomes Betts Pond Road, a point announced by the presence of a stately yet crumbling wood house and the equally mature small barn behind it. The road enters a tunnel of trees, the pines on the left standing between the pavement and a long, meandering pond. I open my window at the start and soon hear the music of water spilling over a low dam. Even on this, the most brilliant of sunlit days,

Betts Pond Road is a shrouded oasis of dense trees, sparkling water, and cool breezes.

If there is any disappointment in Betts Pond Road, it's that this magical length stretches for less than a quarter mile. I turn around and drive it again, and then again, soaking in its gentle curves and shadowy mysteries, reminded of much-longer childhood drives along twisting, narrow roads hugging the shores of New Hampshire lakes.

Delaware returns presently, and now I'm heading north on Patriots Way. I know I need to head east if I'm ever going to find Cape Henlopen.

An ascending plane warns me that I'm getting perilously close to the Georgetown Airport — which makes me as un-lost as I can imagine. Suddenly, crossing Gravel Hill Road, I notice something I've never seen before: a little road peeling off to the left. It's Anderson Corner Road.

The way is pleasingly shaded by forest, inhabited by the occasional ranch house homestead. Pretty soon I spot the delightfully narrow Doddtown Road. It's the best kind of Delaware road: the kind that doesn't even have a center line.

I turn left onto Doddtown, lost again at last.

I'm enjoying this new landscape so much I nearly miss a startling sight to my left: A vast field of trees growing under an equally sprawling series of plastic canopies and arcing PVC frames. I veer off the road and roll past a sign that reads "Shady Oak Farm: Est. 1985."

Each section of the canopied forest is populated by a different kind of small tree or shrub. I can't name any of them, of course, but I recognize them from virtually every yard in front of every house within 20 miles of here.

As I pull up to the office, a friendly guy named Mike hops off a tractor.

"We've got about 22 acres under cover," he says. "It's mostly nuts and bolts shrubbery. Nothing fancy.

"Let me show you something," he says, leading me to a low building at the rear of the property. We push through the door — and before me spread countless tiny plants on tables, shelves, and the floor. This is the cutting room, where baby plants are nurtured year round.

"We've got about 25,000 cuttings in here," says Mike.

In other words, if you own a house in coastal Delaware, chances are your crepe myrtle, holly bush, or English yew started as a sprig in this room.

8. I am lost no more

I head east and find myself on Harbeson Road. Try as I might, I cannot get lost again.

Still, I've set out to go from lighthouse to lighthouse, so I maneuver through Five Points, traffic along Savannah Road, and wind my way through Cape Henlopen State Park.

Not even the sand outcropping that so inefficiently supported the Cape Henlopen beacon remains today. It's a reminder that, if you wait long enough, the sturdiest of landmarks can fade away in a single lifetime. A rotting barn, a fallen oak tree, a vanished field or an extinct strip mall — all are agents of change by subtraction.

So there's hope yet — that after years of living with the constant change that defines coastal Delaware, we may still be able to roam those meandering back roads, and get lost.

FICTION

DON'T PASS ME BY

What a lovely day for a drive, she is thinking. It's a cloudless summer afternoon, and she is on her way home from her pinochle club's covered dish luncheon. She blinks into the sunlight and smiles. Has Lenora Whipple's beer-battered cod left her just a little tipsy?

She noses her gold Chrysler New Yorker onto Robinsonville Road. Her son calls her car the Queen Mary, and she always laughs, but not for the reason he thinks. He doesn't know that he was conceived on the actual Queen Mary in 1946, when she and her husband took that trip to England. Oh, how she loved England. So quaint. Especially the way they drive on the left side of the road. Occasionally, just for fun, she eases the New Yorker across the centerline for awhile, just to relive that wonderful time.

She sees you in her rear view mirror. My, so close! She sees you waving. She slows down to wave back. A good Delaware wave. Now you're waving faster. Oh, do you want her to speed up a bit? Well, she'd honestly love to, but see that sign? Forty-five miles an hour. So sorry! But here, she'll put her left-hand blinker on to show you it's okay to pass.

Here comes Jimtown Road on the right. That name always makes her smile. So friendly. Like everyone in town is named Jim. Hi Jim! Hello Jim! How's your wife Jim and all the little Jims? Jim Dandy, Jim! My word, Jimtown Road has been closed for *months* now. What in the world are they doing there? She slows down to get a good look.

Now you're honking. Oh, she's so sorry! Were you confused because she had her left-hand blinker on and then pulled over to the right?

Here's a nice straightaway. She notices you easing to the left to pass, and begins to feel guilty for going so slow. She hits the gas. Hello, Fifty! But wait — here comes a chicken truck. She hits the brakes, which she always does when facing oncoming traffic. You can't be too careful.

Look at all those poor chickens. She feels bad for them, on their way to being plucked and all. On the other hand, they seem to be enjoying the fresh air. Who knows, this may be the happiest moment of their lives. She smiles and waves at them. A big Delaware wave.

Oh my – construction ahead. There's a nice man holding a stop sign. She rolls to a rest and gives him an extra big Delaware wave. He seems so hot under that heavy yellow vest. When he turns the sign around to "Slow," she pulls up, stops, and hands him a bottle of water she had on the front seat. He's so grateful. His name is Roger, and he says he's working at this because farm jobs are becoming scarce. She suggests that he apply at the chicken plant, because they're always hiring. But Roger likes being outside.

Oh! She was so involved with Roger she nearly forgot you were back there. You and all those other people. She waves to the workers as she carefully negotiates the left lane. Just like England!

Here comes John J Williams Highway, named after that nice man who was our Senator. They called him Honest John.

She sees the traffic light up ahead is green, so she slows down. When the light is green, that means it's going to turn yellow any second, and red right after that.

You're waving again. Hello! She's turning left here, and sees that you're going straight, over to where they're building all those housing developments. Yes, she knows you're here because it's such a lovely place to live, but my goodness, there are so many of you, and you're filling in all the farms and clogging up all our streets.

Anyway, goodbye. She hopes you'll remember to tell all your friends who want to move here about the day she was your Virgil and Robinsonville Road was your own personal circle of Hell.

FINAL APPROACH

He eased the Cessna 172 onto the runway, keeping an eye on the windsock a hundred yards or so to his left. No sign of significant crosswind.

The prevailing wind was from the south, but he'd rolled down this grassy stretch of Eagle Crest aerodrome enough times to know that the field's location, just four miles from the beaches of Delaware, could make for some tricky conditions.

Throttle up, a quick check of the oil pressure and temperature, and he was rolling into the wind. He pulled the control wheel and felt the Cessna rise from the grass. Pointing the plane's nose downward slightly, he set his speed at 75 knots and started to climb.

Ordinarily, he'd be up to 1,000 feet in about a minute, but at 400 he began a long, lazy loop around, heading back toward the field. Below he caught a glimpse of his guys, scrambling in tandem, pulling at a dark rope line and fastening each end to two tall, flexible poles standing on opposite sides of the runway.

He made a low approach, as if coming in for a landing. But he leveled out at about 15 feet, aiming the plane directly between the two poles.

The ground was a blur even at a plodding 75 knots; if he tried to focus on it, he knew he'd get disoriented. Instead he glued his gaze to the stand of trees at the far end of the runway. He was vaguely aware of the two poles whooshing past him on either side, then of a healthy clunk as the hook hanging from his tail caught the line between them.

Now he pulled the plane into a steeper climb, first feeling the drag as the line tugged at his forward progress, then feeling a bump of resistance from the 20-foot advertising banner that he was now towing behind him.

"How's it look? Over," he radioed to the ground.

"Upside-down! Over," came the response. Then a laugh.

They always said that when everything was fine. He chuckled and wanted to respond with a choice good-natured profanity or two, but you just don't do that on these frequencies. They don't kid around at the FAA.

Besides, this was the best part, watching the quilt work of lower Delaware spread below him. As he banked to the northeast, passing over the ribbon of Route 1 (and those poor suckers who get around on four wheels instead of two wings) he could see the green wilderness of Prime Hook and the late morning sun illuminating the twisting course of the Broadkill River. The brilliant glare progressed along the river's entire length, visible from end to end, as if the water itself had been set afire. From up here he marveled, as always, at how the preserve was more water than not, a great damp doormat of grassy bottomland. He had canoed and kayaked down there many times, veering from the broad waterway whenever he could, ducking as he pushed his low-floating craft into forbidden zones of chattering wildlife.

The beach soon passed beneath him, followed by the expanse of the Delaware Bay. He lifted his eyes to the horizon and saw the ferry churning its way to New Jersey. Why do people even go to New Jersey, he wondered. Of course, to judge by the housing developments erupting as far as he could see, it was clear that the balance of ferry passengers was definitely tipping in favor of the Cape May-to-Lewes crowd. In a few years, he suspected, the ferry would forever be heading to New Jersey empty, only to refill with beleaguered Jersey refugees.

He loved to go high, as high as his Cessna would take him. Which isn't all that high — not when you compare it to the heights he used to reach during his Air Force years. In the Cessna, the entire bowl of sky remains the blue of a baby's eyes — nothing like when you pierce the atmosphere's veil in an F-16. Up there, where the air is barely thick enough to lift your wings, the sky shines bright blue near the horizon, then fades to gray. And above you — well, sometimes you can imagine yourself just hitting the jets into that darkening blackness and sending yourself into orbit.

But this was not a day to go high. Not even a little high. Nor fast. The folks down there on the beach should not need binoculars to read that sign you're dragging back there. Nor should they require speed-reading skills to comprehend it.

No, a nice steady 75 knots was just about right, about 250 feet up and 1,000 feet from shore.

He buzzed passed lazy Lewes Beach and traced a wide arc around the sandy scythe of Cape Henlopen. Along the coast, fishermen sat on lounge chairs behind their fat-tired SUVs, some of them actually fishing.

He was glad to have the air space today; too often recently, he'd had to cede it to those orange Coast Guard helicopters that patrol the shoreline without explanation. What are they looking for? These waters seem unlikely targets for invasion, he thought — ironically, just as he was passing the cylindrical concrete observation tower at the tip of the cape. Ahead, jutting from the sands between Gordon's Pond and the Atlantic, stood two more of them, sentries that protected the Delaware River from the very real threat of German U-boats. Ah well, let the Coast Guard have its right of way, he thought. They're not that bad for business.

It was a busy day on Rehoboth's beach. The hot sand was cooling beneath a canopy of blue-and-white umbrellas. Here and there he could spot people waving to him. He waved back, although he knew full well they could never see him. Occasionally little kids would start running along the water's edge, legs pistoning, arms pumping wildly, trying to keep up. For them, he'd dip his wing slightly, being careful not to let his banner go slack.

The radiant orange-red Dolle's Saltwater Taffy sign slid by. He could see the garage doors rolling up at Funland, and he wished he were flying here in the late evening when the lights of the rides lend a Coney Island vibe to the scene.

Next came the two-mile length of private beach homes — dead space for the advertisers paying for that banner. Slim chance that the owners of these conspicuous supershacks were inclined to take advantage of a $5 margarita happy hour.

The Dewey Beach crowd, however, perked up visibly as he passed overhead. Nearing the end of their beach week, they had by now sated themselves at The Rusty Rudder and Bottle N' Cork, and they were on the lookout for one more watering hole before heading back to their lousy, landlubbing lives.

The state beach came into view and, beyond that, the quad spires of the Indian River Inlet bridge. His contract did not require him to venture any farther south — no sense pushing happy hour on the horseshoe crab population. So he swung inland and headed back north, following the line of Route 1, out of sight of the beach, ducking backstage before re-entering from stage right.

Three passes and it was time to change out the banner. He curled north one last time and climbed, avoiding the brunt of an offshore breeze. Up here, at 1,000 feet, the air actually felt lighter. He held his nose and popped his ears.

That's when he saw them: Three wedges of Canadian geese heading in the same direction he was, cruising along a few hundred feet below. He didn't even think; he'd heard of pilots doing this, and he wanted to know what it was like. He lowered the Cessna's nose, powered himself in their direction, and cut the engine.

He was gliding. The propeller in front of him slowed, then began to spin powerlessly, pushed only by the wind. At first he was conscious solely of the rush of air around the cockpit and the soft whistle of air playing on his wing support struts. Powerless flight was a mandatory step in the pilot training process, so he'd heard these sounds and felt the dramatic change in the feel of his instruments before. But this time there was an added element: The approaching cacophony of honks wafting his way from the squadron of Canadian geese.

The Cessna slid into formation, taking position roughly in the middle of a large goosey chevron. He looked from side to side, half expecting the birds to crane their necks in his direction, taking measure of this ungainly interloper. But the geese seemed unperturbed. Their necks stayed ramrod straight, their doll-like eyes focused on some undisclosed destination directly ahead.

But the sound! At first the honking seemed random, chaotic. But soon audible patterns developed as the birds seemed to throw fragments of staccato conversation to each other, a sort of call-and-response chorus that tossed itself from left to right, front to back, and then the whole thing in reverse. Were they talking about him? Were they figuring a strategy for shaking this unwelcome hanger-on? Or were they shouts of welcome?

And there was something else: All around swirled a murmur of beating wings, moving the muffled air with an insistence that reminded him of a field of ruffling flags.

He had to admit to himself he was never a fan of Canadian geese. They mucked up the streets and sidewalks of his neighborhood and soiled the water catchment pond behind his house. But up here, on this morning, he was in their realm. He felt at home.

He was also drawing a little too close to the point of the wedge. Time to bow out. He lowered the Cessna's elevators and dipped downward, out of the birds' line of flight. At an appropriate distance, he flipped the master switch, opened the throttle, and turned the Cessna's key to the right.

Nothing happened.

The propeller continued its lethargic spin; the wind kept whistling by. But as for the familiar sputter and start of the Cessna's engine, the absence of those sounds made the cockpit seem as silent as a tomb.

He was flying dead-stick, at the mercy of the wind, updrafts, and gravity.

A sharp thwack on his windshield punctured the unwelcome silence. He stared dumbly at the black-and-blue smear spreading there. A goose had left him a good-bye gift.

From this altitude, he couldn't quite make out the Eagle's Nest Aerodrome, but his instruments assured him he was heading on a straight line toward it. He was glad he'd ascended as high as he did, less pleased that he'd sacrificed so much elevation to get to goose level. But as he eyeballed the landmarks below, he felt reasonably certain his home runway was within reach. The field had no tower, but with two turf runways, he was pretty sure he'd find one free and clear of traffic.

The Tanger Outlets were passing below. Did his wife tell him she was going to be stopping there this morning? He wished he'd paid more attention. Ridiculously, he scanned the parking lot of the Bayside mall, wondering if he might spot her white Mazda.

He opened his radio frequency and raised the guys at the aerodrome. He alerted them to his predicament, carefully avoiding any indication of how he'd come to be in this ridiculous position. No sense putting that over the airwaves. He'd have enough questions to answer when it was all over.

Something didn't seem right. Well, nothing seemed right, actually, but there was something definitely squirrelly going on with his descent. As he passed over the perpetual traffic jam at Five Points, the ground seemed to be coming up entirely too fast. His altimeter was rapidly slipping lower, even though he had a decent tail wind and the paved-over landscape of the Route 1 business district was providing a stellar updraft.

He rolled his eyes and threw his head back. Of course! The banner! Idiot, he thought. Flying with that fluttering albatross was like dragging an anchor behind a cruise ship. Instantly he yanked on the release handle and felt the Cessna pop forward, like a car that's suddenly lost its trailer. The banner billowed into the distance. He imagined some guy wandering into his back yard to find, draped over his barbecue, a 20-foot-long invitation to early evening drinks.

It was better, but the damage had been done. The aerodrome seemed a distant impossibility. The altimeter showed he was below 500 feet. Still, as he'd discovered when he'd practiced them before, dead-stick landings are surprisingly simpler than powered ones. No concerns about throttle. No monitoring air speed. Just keep the thing straight and steer for the flat place. Any flat place.

He voice activated his cell phone. She picked up immediately. Was everything okay? It sounded awfully quiet. No, everything was fine. He was headed back to the airport.

Just wanted to say hi. Thanks for this morning. Looking forward to dinner. I love you. 'Bye.

Beyond that stand of trees, he knew, was a cow pasture. Almost as good as the aerodrome — flat and grassy. He pulled up, easing the Cessna over the stand like a deer clearing a hedge. But instead of a pasture, he discovered a Jenga-like collection of half-built homes.

He frowned. When did *that* happen? The situation was hairy, and getting hairier by the moment. The house skeletons seemed to reach up for him, trying to wrap their woody fingers around the Cessna's wheels. The ground was now a senseless blur. Grass and pavement. Rocks and road.

Dairy Farm Road. It's straight, it's not heavily traveled, and it's right behind me, he thought. Smoothly turning the wheel and pressing the rudder pedal, he banked to the left. His wing barely cleared a power line. Now he was facing the wind; light, but enough to force him to recalculate his chances of making it the quarter mile or so along Sweet Briar Road, zipping along below him, to the Dairy Farm Road straightaway just beyond Route 9. He'd be landing right here, on Sweet Briar.

The road was largely clear, except for a pickup truck heading in the same direction he was. He held his breath as the Cessna's wheels barely cleared the vehicle roof. Above the rushing wind, he heard the driver swear, heard the screeching of his wheels as he hit his brakes and the truck fishtailed to a stop.

The road rose to meet him, and it wasn't any Irish blessing.

About 30 yards from the Route 9 intersection, his wheels touched pavement. He yanked the flaps full open, desperately hoping to maintain a straight line. Cars zipped across the street in front of him — the drivers and passengers staring in stupefied horror at the single-engine plane that threatened to t-bone them.

To avoid entering the busy intersection, he was fully prepared to slam the brakes which would inevitably cause the Cessna to flip forward, and then who knew what.

Then the traffic light turned green.

He couldn't believe his good fortune. Rattling and groaning against the pavement, the Cessna rolled south through the intersection like a winged SUV.

He gently applied the brake. The Cessna rolled past the parking lot of the Hopkins Dairy ice cream stand and ambled off the road at the point where it makes a slight left turn — the beginning of the straightaway he'd been aiming for.

It came to a stop, about 20 yards short of a small herd of cows. They ignored him, except for one who turned her head lazily, blinked slowly, then resumed whatever conversation she was having with her sister cows.

He sat there, soaking in the silence. Somewhere, someone mooed.

He sighed. Pushing the Cessna door open, he climbed out, feasting on the feel of ground beneath his feet. He trudged back to the dairy store, past the gaping faces of two families who'd stopped for what they'd expected would be an uneventful ice cream outing. Their mouths hung open, as if they'd forgotten how to complete the act of licking their rocky road sugar cones.

From behind the small window marked *Order Here*, a girl, fifteen or so, stared at him. He looked at her for a while, his mouth tight.

"I'd like a chocolate malt," he finally said.

The girl managed to croak out, "What size?"

He narrowed his eyes and cast them across the parking lot. The tail of the Cessna was just visible above a Dodge Caravan.

"Large," he said. "Make it a large."

He was sitting on the top of a picnic table, his feet resting on the seat, sucking down his chocolate malt when he felt her presence. She slid next to him on the table, joining the vigil as he stared at the incongruous Cessna.

"We've lived here for what, 25 years?" he asked, maintaining his gaze. "In all that time, have we *ever* made the light at Route 9 and Dairy Farm?"

She shook her head.

"No, I didn't think so." He turned to her. "How did you find me?"

"Find My Friends," she said, pulling her smart phone from her jeans pocket. On the screen were their two icons, nesting together like the sun and the moon in partial eclipse, at Hopkins Dairy.

He squinted to the south and gestured toward the Dairy Farm Road straightaway. "You know," he said, "once I get that engine working, I could just take off that way."

She took the malt from his hands, put the straw to her lips, and nodded.

A NOTE AT THE END

Well, see, that wasn't so bad now, was it? Thanks for sticking with me — I was afraid I'd lose you back there at the pond guy, but you persevered and good for you! Besides, I loved that pond guy.

Speaking of whom, I would be remiss to not personally thank all the people who let me interview them for the magazine articles that informed this book. I would seriously love to give each of you a complimentary copy, but there's a statistical chance that there are more people in this book than will actually buy this book, and that's no kind of business model.

Thanks to Tom Kavanaugh, editor *par excellence*, whose deft touch improved each magazine article he handled. Trust me, if you found a typo or garbled syntax somewhere in this book, that was a passage Tom never laid eyes on.

Finally and most emphatically, infinite thanks to the astonishing Carolyn Newcott, who with infinite patience and inexplicable devotion summoned every sinew of her long experience editing encyclopedias to re-read every word of the final draft. She never fails to make me better at everything I do, and also look better than I actually am.

About The Author

BILL NEWCOTT lived in the Bronx just long enough (one week) to say he was born in the Bronx. Educated in the finest private school Dumont, NJ, had to offer, he was pleased to learn that the farther away he got from his collegiate alma mater, Rutgers University, the better its reputation became (Upon landing his first newspaper job near Los Angeles, CA, he was happy to learn Californians considered Rutgers to be "Ivy League"). In LA he won the UPI Western States Feature Writing Award (1979); the following year he went to work for *The National Enquirer*, where by the time he escaped a decade later he'd risen to the post of Associate Editor. Ten years at *National Geographic* magazine ensued; there he shamelessly wrote more byline articles than anyone else had scored in the magazine's previous 110 years. As space science editor, he won the 1996 Aviation Space Writers Association award for excellence. A move to *AARP the Magazine* led to his longest professional tenure (18 years) during which he served as entertainment and travel editor and created the influential Movies For Grownups Awards. There he won numerous Mature Media Awards for his efforts, along with a Lowell Thomas Award for Best Travel Coverage and a Gracie Award for his long-running *Movies For The Rest of Us* radio show, heard weekly on 600 stations. Currently, he is the a award-winning film critic for *The Saturday Evening Post* and contributes to numerous outlets including *Delaware Beach Life*, *National Geographic*, Fodor's and various regional travel magazines. The International Regional Magazine Association named him 2020 writer of the year. His previous books include *100 Must-See Movies For Grownups* and *The National Geographic Expeditions Atlas*.

Most pieces in this book were first published, in slightly or largely different form, in *Delaware Beach Life* magazine:

"Vulture Culture" November 2018; "Into the Sunsets" July 2018; "Goin' to the Chapels" November 2018; "The Christmas Tree Farmers" November 2018; "Let's Get High" April 2020; "The Boardwalk Guy" April 2019; "Tall, Dark and Handsome" April 2019; "Catch the Wave" June 2019; "The Bra Fitter" June 2019; "Mind the Gap" May 2019; "The Ferry Captain" May 2019; "The Disney Next Door" July 2019 "The Crab Pot Cop" July 2019; "Signs of the Times" July 2019; "The Treasure Hunter" October 2019; "The Ghosts at the Cafe" October 2019; "Putt 'er There" September 2019; "The Movie Maven" September 2019; "The K-9 Team" August 2019; "Think Tank" August 2019; "A Load of Bull" November 2019; "The Boat Builders" November 2020; "House of Future Past" September 2019; "Let Us Spray" November 2019; "Getting Lost" April 2020; "Rocks of Ages" September 2020; "The Pond Guy" May 2020; "A State of Bee-Ing" May 2020; "The Aerodrome Manager" April 2020; "The Telescope in the Cemetery" August 2020: "Roll-Up Retreats" November 2020; "The Roadside Environmentalist" November 2020: "Zoltar's Father" June 2020; "The Music Makers" June 2020: "The Pest Management Specialist" June 2020: "The Well Driller" July 2020; "The Tree in the '62 Chevy" June 2020; "The Taxidermist" October 2020; "The Ghost of Fiddler's Hill" October 2020; "Sex and the Single Alpaca" September 2020; "Making Tracks" September 2020; "A Fish Poops in Selbyville" April 2021; "Where the Bodies Are Buried" May 2021; "The Dairy Farmer" May 2021

"Final Approach" was originally published in *Scenes: A Collaboration of Coastal Writers and Artists* (2019, The Rehoboth Beach Writers' Guild)

Made in the USA
Middletown, DE
19 June 2021

42513933R00156